Creation and Human Dynamism

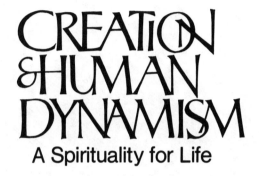

CREATION & HUMAN DYNAMISM

A Spirituality for Life

Joseph G. Donders

TWENTY-THIRD PUBLICATIONS
Mystic, Connecticut

Twenty-Third Publications
P.O. Box 180
Mystic, CT 06355
(203) 536-2611

Library of Congress Catalog Card Number 85-50689
ISBN paper: 0-89622-250-0
      cloth: 0-89622-227-6

Edited by Louise Pittaway
Cover Design by George Herrick
Designed by Andrea Star

Preface

The intention in writing this book is to redirect the reader to the most fundamental issue in the Bible: creation. It is also the first issue presented to us in the Bible. The story of creation is the story of creating human life. Air, light, the sun and moon, earth and water, plants and animals are all planned and created in view of human life.

While creating, God is opting for human life. In a sense, God's creative impulse ended at the moment Adam and Eve embraced each other for the first time. At that point they accepted God's option and became carriers of God's creative impulse. The continuation of that choice is variously described throughout the rest of the Bible. Its full acceptance came with Jesus Christ.

It is in the acceptance of that same divine option that our human future lies. It is in the working out of that choice in our personal and communal life that our human life finds its destiny.

I would like to thank the Reverend Harry van Pelt, Chief Editor of the Altiora Press of the Norbertine Abbey, Averbode in Belgium, who gave permission to use in this book some material published in the *Cahiers voor levensverdieping*.

Thanks is also due to Ms. Rosemary Barwa who diligently typed the manuscript.

Saint Paul Chaplaincy
University of Nairobi
Nairobi, Kenya, Africa

CONTENTS

Part I

THE OLD TESTAMENT

and

CREATION

1

Desacralization of the World's Reality

The word secularization does not sound pleasant. It definitely does not sound pretty in religious ears. It indicates that something holy lost its sacred character. It points at a desacralization, a subtraction, a diminishment.

The word was not born in pleasant circumstances either. It was originally used to indicate that one or another ecclesiastical possession—an orchard, a house, livestock, a service, a school, or university—was taken away from church ownership. Such a removal always meant a loss from the church's point of view.

In that sense the word is still often used in church circles. It is used to indicate the general contemporary tendency to desacralize so much of what was holy to earlier generations. Many sigh that marriage, family life, and human relations in general have lost their sacred character. Others lament that our modern social system has desacralized the works of mercy. Some complain that the sacredness of prayer has given way to secularized meditation and other psychological gadgets and techniques. Many worry that everything has been "secularized." It is as if someone has removed every sacred, pious, or religious dimension from the world. Everything is profaned and nothing has depth or deeper dimension.

The process of secularization has everything in its grip. What remains? It is about that remainder that we would like to reflect in this book. Before we do, the process of secularization must be analyzed more carefully. What really did happen?

At first sight, the desacralization of the world's reality seems to be something impious, something almost blasphemous, until we remember that many stories in the Old Testament had exactly that purpose. They were told to desacralize realities in this world. The difference between the Hebrews and the surrounding pagans was precisely that the Hebrews were not allowed to worship all kinds of things that the pagans adored both day and night.

Desacralizing the Moon

The process of secularization starts with Abram, father of the biblical belief in God. He is the first human being whom we can place historically in the biblical stories; that is to say, we have been able to excavate the environment in which he lived.

According to the first biblical reports, Abram lived with his father Terach in Ur, one of the oldest cities in history, founded about three thousand years before the birth of Christ.

At a certain point, Terach and his son Abram decided to leave Ur. It is not mentioned in the Old Testament why they left. There is, however, a legend to be found in the pseudepigrapha Book of Jubilees. In that legend there is a hint that the two had to leave because Abram had desecrated the local temple where children were often sacrificed.

This temple, dedicated to the moon, as we know from excavations, housed an idol—a small blue statue of an elderly bearded man. He was called Sin by the inhabitants of Ur.

Terach and Abram migrated to Charan. There, too, the same moon-god was venerated. The cult of the moon was something very common among agricultural peoples, there being a very clear relationship between the moon and fertility. Even today it is said that more babies are born on the nights of the full moon than on any other night. In many places around the world, farmers traditionally take the moon's phases into account when sowing their crops.

But Abram had to leave Charan, too. His god, the idol his wife was carrying in her saddlebag, inspired him to go away and to break with that older belief. He had to liberate himself from the moon. To him that planet was no longer a deity or anything sacred and holy. He went. People must have considered him an atheist and a blasphemer.

Desacralizing Human Sacrifice

Abram took a further step. He finally sired a son with his wife, Sarah. He named him Isaac (meaning laughter) because his wife had laughed so much when she was told in her old age that she would have a son. It was her firstborn.

Isaac was born in a region where it was customary to sacrifice first fruits to the one considered to be the Holy Other One, Mother Nature. To be assured of further blessings, the first fruits had to be offered to her. This terrible custom was practiced not only in Canaan but also in many other regions in the world.

It might have been under the pressure of that custom that Abram climbed with Isaac to the top of the sacrificial mountain. There, as he was about to sacrifice his son, he was told that God did not want that type of sacrifice. Abram was again liberated from an old fear. His God desacralized nature in so far as birth and fertility were concerned. Contrary to all kinds of other sacred powers, Abram's God did not want human life sacrificed to him.

Abram's God wanted Isaac to live. When Abram returned from the mountain with his son alive, the people must have considered him an atheist, as one without respect for religious customs.

Desacralizing the Sun

The descendants of Abram (who is now called Abraham by God to signify his change in status as father of many nations) proceeded on the same road and in the same direction. They, too, undid the sacredness of all kinds of nondivine realities around them. They have continued to do this even to our day. Didn't Marx secularize money and capital; Freud tap untouchable realms of the human mind; and Einstein upset our almost sacred ideas of time and space?

It would be impossible to repeat here all of the secularizing stories of the Old Testament. Let us restrict ourselves to some core reports. Take the story of Joseph and his colorful dreamcoat. Joseph had always been a dreamer, even after his sale as a slave to Egypt by his envious brothers. In Egypt he became aware of something very strange while interpreting the dreams of others.

He was not astonished that he had discovered, while interpreting the dreams of Pharaoh, how the river Nile would be the cause of seven lean years after seven fat years because of its low water level. He was, however, astonished at how the Egyptians, who considered the river divine, acquiesced to its whims. The only thing one could do was to bring sacrifices to the river. For the rest, one respected the caprices of that power of nature.

Joseph proposed to build barns to store grain during the abundant years. Through the construction of those barns, he ended the superstitious Egyptian dependency on the Nile. Again a Hebrew desacralized something very holy. Humanity became more independent, more self-reliant, more itself. There was sufficient food for everyone during the lean years, not only for the Egyptians but even for the Hebrew people who migrated to Egypt for that food.

Once in Egypt, the Hebrews escaped from their dependency on the moon but were caught by another old divine power, especially venerated by warring and hunting people: the sun.

Pharaoh justified his absolute power over the Egyptian people, and later over the Hebrew people by appealing to the idea of his relationship to the sun. He was the son of the sun. That is why one carried two half circles of ostrich feathers behind him wherever he appeared in public. (Ironically, later popes had those same two half circles carried behind them when they appeared in public. It was Pope John XXIII who abolished that old pagan custom.)

It was the great prophet Moses who, inspired and commanded by the God of Abraham, liberated his people from that primeval idolatrous power. It was at the feet of Pharaoh that the struggle between the old gods and Abraham's God was decided. The old lost, the new won.

The New Place of Human Life

Within the "new," God had been the cause of a new impulse in our world. In all the stories of the Old Testament, it was God who took the initiative. God made humanity emancipate. God liberated humanity from old bonds and spells. The human being became more and more itself, and more and more the center of all and everything. These stories reached their climax during the time of Moses. In that time God's development-aid reached a peak.

A law given by Moses to his people in the name of God was not something extraordinary. The same also happened among the peoples who surrounded them. Within the law Moses gave, however, was one element that was very striking for the time and age in which he lived—an element one might call, without exaggeration, unique, and one by which the secularizing tendency in regard to nature was going to be more stimulated than ever before.

The beginning phrase of the law given by Moses was: I am the Lord your God. Within the biblical tradition, there was absolutely no doubt about that. God *is*, and God is *our Lord*. If one does not accept this reality, one steps out of the biblical tradition.

This experience and this belief, however, do not form the unique character of the ten commandments. That uniqueness is expressed in the following prohibition: Don't make an image of me!

The impact of those words often escapes us. God is, and yet we are not allowed to form an image of him. The Hebrews were allowed to see nothing as an image of God, not the moon or the sun, or anything else. They would never be allowed to dance piously and religiously before an image of God, either made by themselves or taken from nature. Any image was forbidden and excluded. Nothing in nature was allowed to be a carrier of divinity. The Hebrews stood religiously empty-handed in their faith.

Even when they built a temple, though that had never been the intention of their God, that temple seemed to be empty in the eyes of the pagan tourists. There was no image of God in that temple. There was nothing but an empty space between the hands of the cherubim.

Yet, that was not the whole story. In the temple stood the tabernacle in which lay the two stone tablets where the ten commandments were supposedly kept. Those two stone tablets not only told the people that they should not make an image of God; they also told them that, in the name of that God, *human life* had to be taken as the center of their interest and worship: Honor your father and your mother, build an honest society, take care of good relationships between men and women, never kill, and so on. The tablets also mentioned a one-day rest every week in honor of God.

From the Beginning

This kind of development had been the issue since Abraham's departure from Ur. In those days God had already chosen to support human life. In the ten commandments, humanity is asked to do the same. When a pious Jew in front of the Tabernacle would ask almighty God what he should do, he received the same answer Jesus later gave to the question: Love God, who in the name of your love for him, asks you to put humanity in the center of your love.

It is often said by atheists that people who believe in God cannot take humanity seriously at the same time. To believe in God would mean to be alienated from oneself.

Karl Marx thought that any critique of religion should end with the avowal that the human being is the highest reality; and for that reason, all relations in which humankind is humiliated, frustrated, diminished, or enslaved should be abandoned. He included in this abandonment the religious relationships to a God as well.

Marx did not comprehend the core of the Judaeo-Christian tradition. Most probably, he could not understand it, living in the religious and ecclesiastical environment in which he did. In that milieu, humanity was too often oppressed in the name of the Judaeo-Christian belief. Yet, it is precisely

the God of that tradition who offers the only guarantee for
what Marx and so many others wanted to realize.

Humanity lives in the permanent and acute danger of
sacrificing itself to something outside itself that it considers
absolute. A human experience, returning again and again in
history, is that of a greater, more holy dimension. Every
human being knows that he or she is not absolute. Thus
everyone seeks to clarify the Other absolute. The Other can
mean a great danger. How do we visualize that Other One?
Again and again people generate an image of that Other.
They focus on one or another idea or image to be the
absolute.

Sometimes the absolute was a race or a tribe; other
times, blood or soil. Now and then it was a material idol: a
career, car, or other possession. Again and again, humans
sacrifice themselves and their fellow beings to such a Moloch.
This development not only takes place in the reality of human
history, it has also frequently been the topic of stories and
plays in which authors reveal and clarify the other. It is one
of the main topics in the books of a Nobel Prize winner for
literature, William Golding.

In his most famous book, *The Lord of the Flies*, a large
passenger plane broke in half above a deserted island somewhere in the Pacific. The plane had been flying a group of boys
back to their boarding school. The entire adult crew died in
the crash. Their part of the plane disappeared into the ocean.

The boys, in the second part of the plane landed more
or less safely on the beach of the island. One member of the
crew, the pilot, had initially been able to escape, too. But he
ended up in a tree, and remained hanging there until he died.

Left to their own devices, the boys began a new society. Originally they even hoped to make it better than any
society that had existed before—a dream that enchants most
of us at some stage of our lives. Soon, it became obvious that
they would not be able to succeed. All of the old human ills
began to develop among them.

They started to look for the Other, some absolute who
would be mightier than they were and who would be able to
help them.

The boys found the dead and decomposing pilot hanging in the tree. They organized a kind of liturgy around him; and in one of their celebrations, a small fat boy disappeared. Sacrificed to that Other One? No one really knew. They found only his pair of glasses after the ceremony.

The Other One in the Jewish tradition—God—made it clear from the very beginning that such a liturgy should not be organized. God made himself known as one who condemns all human sacrifice. God does not want humanity to sacrifice itself to him. He wants the human being to be, to live. Humanity was not allowed to render that kind of "honor" to anyone, or anything, in a world declared secularized by God.

At the moment the Hebrews again began that type of sacrifice, when they again began to offer their children on the hilltops of their land, they committed the most serious sin possible, and immediately they were threatened by their prophets.

The nadir in this sinfulness was reached by them just before the Babylonian exile, when they decided in a meeting of all the people to return to the worship of the old powers of nature—the Queen of Heaven, a Canaanite deity. They turned away from the God of Abraham, Isaac, and Jacob, in spite of the warnings of Jeremiah.

Jeremiah asked them to reconsider, but (the men) answered: We refuse to listen to what you have told us in the name of the Lord. We will do everything that we said we would. We will offer sacrifices to our goddess, the Queen of Heaven, and we will pour out wine offerings to her just as we and our ancestors, our king and our leaders used to do in the towns of Judah and in the streets of Jerusalem. Then we had plenty of food; we were prosperous and had no troubles. But ever since we stopped sacrificing to the Queen of Heaven and stopped pouring out wine offerings to her, we have had nothing, and our people have died in war and starvation. And the women added: When we baked cakes shaped like the Queen of Heaven, offered sacrifices to her and poured out wine offerings to her, our husbands approved of what we were doing.

At the moment they began to see those powers of nature as sacred again, they not only lost sight of God, but also lost sight of their own sacredness and integrity. In fact the secularization of the world had meant, at the same time, the sacralization of humanity. God had asked them to honor themselves and nothing else.

Exile Reflections

Slowly, those initially very strange secularizing thoughts began to be understood. When Abraham's descendants began to reflect upon their history in the misery of the exile, they began to realize what God's intention had been from the very beginning.

In that spirit they began to record their stories about the beginning. In those stories, God created humanity as the main reality in creation. The human being is created with the mission to grow outward; and to be able to do that, the rest of creation is given to help in that growth, a job- and life-description God would repeat to Noah and his children after the great flood.

People understood by then that God was not interested in a temple of stone in his honor. God's temple was humanity—the human beings living from the very beginning with the breath of life that God had blown into their nostrils. We often overlook the importance of that first puff of divine breath, that first puff of Divine Spirit into us. The breath was not only given to Adam and Eve, it was given to each human being. That Spirit is still within us. Nothing we need has come from outside; it must come from within. The Spirit has to be brought to light within us.

A Parallel Development

During this process, the Hebrew people were led back to their beginning, to their creational origin. At the same time, something else became clear to them. The Almighty Other, who originally was seen as a mother by the whole of humanity, a mother taking care of everything, was now being seen as having "fatherly" characteristics as well.

God was seen as taking care in a different way. He ruled not only from somewhere "above," he began to entrust the whole of nature with all its possibilities and powers to humanity. It is in that way that humanity grew. Through his care, we became more and more self-reliant and responsible.

Initially, all kinds of events were still directly attributed to God. It was God who sent the quails into camp when there was no meat to eat. It was God who provided the manna every morning. It was God who beat the enemies when his people called for help like small children in the street shouting, "Wait, I am going to call my parents, and you will see what happens!"

It began slowly to dawn on them that the real center of God's attention was not only on the people of Israel, but on the whole of humanity. That must have been understood by them when they reported the creation story as they did. Not only the Israelites, but all of humanity was created by God. He was father to all nations.

All of these ideas grew slowly. What God had asked humanity to do, in the law of Moses, and in the story of creation—to take humanity as the center of our interest—was definitively realized when God became our brother in Jesus Christ. It is only Jesus who would dare to pronouce that radical word "Father" when speaking about God. In him a new period began. In Jesus, God was standing next to us as one of us.

Notwithstanding his geographical and historical restrictions, Jesus made it very clear that he was there for Jew, Greek, Samaritan, pagan, the rich and the poor, the sinner and the saint, for friend and enemy. His interest went out not only to a small group, to an elite, it went out to all humanity.

2

Creation:
Option for Human Life

Adam and Eve embraced each other, and God withdrew. God went, writes the Bible, to take a rest from his creative work. God's creative dynamism had been passed on to those two human beings, representing and containing the whole of humanity.

In few books further along in the Bible, the same responsibility is stressed in another way. In chapter thirty of the Book of Deuteronomy, Moses tells the Hebrew people that they have to choose between good and evil, between life and death. All human life derives from God's original option for that life and from the further choice of all our forefathers and foremothers, our ancestors who, in their turn, opted for that life, and out of whom we all are born.

The issue of that story in Deuteronomy is not only life without further ado. It is not only a question of survival, of begetting children. It is also about a certain quality of life, its organization and its interpretations. In other words, it concerns human culture and human adventure.

What was begun by the power of God in a dynamic way had to be "formed" in order to be able to continue to develop. God not only gave life; but from the very beginning, he gave that life a quality. The authors of the Bible express that idea in a remark God made after each creative explosion.

Looking back on the work of each day, God repeats

that the results of his work are "good." The word good here
has no moral meaning. It has a creational meaning; it expresses
a kind of guarantee, a hallmark, a kind of trademark. It is
about a quality that cannot be undone. "God created all
things that they might have being. The creative forces of the
word make for life; there is no deadly poison in them"
(Wisdom 1:14-15).

Bonhoeffer wrote: "The goodness indicated here con-
sists in the fact that creation is God's work."[1] It is a goodness
that cannot be lost in which everything, but especially
everyone, still participates at this very moment. It is that
goodness that made every human population group choose
life. It is on that dynamism that all existing human cultures
are based. It is for this reason that all those cultures deserve
our respect.

When Christians condemn other cultures as totally
wrong, or even as satanic, they make a very serious mistake
— a mistake by which one opts against forms of life that had
been chosen by those non-Christian groups from within their
divine creative dynamism.

One can find in all cultures superstitious theories and
practices that go against the original option for, and faith in,
life. Those superstitions can also be found in our Western
Christian context, as we will see in the next chapter. Every
culture has to be studied critically from this point of view.
That critique should try to ascertain the where and how of *life
for all*.

The story of creation considers human life and its
dynamics as one whole. The report speaks of Adam and Eve
as starting the human family. According to that story, the
breath, that "kiss of life" God blew into the nostrils of
Adam and Eve is the breath with which all human beings are
still living. The Bible story is about *the life of all*. This fact
goes unnoticed by most in our world today. We forget that
creation is "for all." Consider for a moment these figures
and these anomalies.

At present six million Europeans eat as much food as
two hundred forty million Africans (6,000,000:240,000,000).
A Canadian eats seventy times more than an inhabitant of

Upper Volta, a country in West Africa (70:1). The citizens of the United States of America, who form only 5.7% of the world's population, eat half the food produced in the world. The so-called Western part of the world spends ten times more money on the feeding of cats and dogs than the sovereign country, Guinea, earns as its national income. There are only four countries in Africa whose national income is higher than the amount of money spent on cattle fodder in the USA. And, yet, it is in the West that one hears, "They should be sterilized in the Third World; they are getting too numerous, and there is not enough food for all of us."

What was observed about food, is, of course, also applicable to clothing, water, shelter, and education. It is no exaggeration to say that practically 80 percent of the Africans are walking around in second-hand clothing from the West, imported by unscrupulous dealers. The existing differences are sometimes ridiculous and are, at the same time, sad and incomprehensible.

At times, the absurdity of inequalities is revealed in unexpected ways. A student-chaplain at the University of Nairobi, Kenya, received a letter from a university in Pennsylvania asking him whether it would be possible for a student from that university to get into contact with a group of Africans threatened by starvation. The student would then, after having stayed for a year in such a group, return to the USA to report on his experiences during "dinner-dialogues." The sponsors were willing to spend 25,000 U.S. dollars on that project. One would be able to pay about 100 Kenyans the official minimum salary for a full year with that amount of money! These differences make the creative dynamism in our world dangerous and bring about many tensions.

Those differences hinder the possibility of a harmonious community. The world is divided over interest groups profiting as much as possible. The attempt to organize an optimal quality of life for all is no more than a joke. In older, more traditional human life groups, those differences would not have been allowed.

In many regions of Africa, a house that was larger

than those normally built would be torn down—the community members would not permit such a difference. They were afraid of those inequalities which they knew would ruin society and would finally lead to bloodshed. They tried to organize a life style within their communities that would offer a maximum of life quality to all.

We often think, and say, that the simplicity of life in the Third World is due to underdevelopment. It is, however, possible to look at that simplicity from a totally different point of view. To ensure a good life to as many as possible and, if possible, to all, the life-communities within the Third World often purposely opted for that simple lifestyle. Its simplicity made life feasible for all the community members. It prevented differences and the consequences of inequalities.

When those inequalities are permitted, they call to heaven for revenge; they askew creation's dynamism. The "for all" becomes a "for me," a new and dangerous idol!

God Favors the Oppressed

If God really opts for human life, then it becomes unavoidable that God will be especially interested in those whose lives are frustrated. It is a logical consequence. It is a logic that is true of ourselves. Our hands go out to the part of our body that is suffering, stiff, or tired. When my left knee hurts, my special attention will go out to that left knee, and most probably I will be sitting with that knee in my hands.

This preference of God is reported to us in many stories of the Bible. The main story of this type is, of course, the report of the exodus from Egypt, summarized shortly and powerfully in Deuteronomy 26:5-9.

> My ancestor was a wandering Aramean, a homeless refugee, who took his family to Egypt to live. They were few in number when they went there, but they became a large and powerful nation. The Egyptians treated us harshly and forced us to work as slaves. Then we cried out for help to the Lord, the God of our ancestors. He heard us and saw our suffering, hardship, and misery. He

worked miracles and wonders, and caused terrify-
ing things to happen. He brought us here and gave
us this rich and fertile land.

The Egyptians tried to steal life itself away from the
Hebrews, according to the same reports, by murdering all
male infants immediately after their birth. God's creative
work was frustrated in a shocking way. How could it be
possible that he would tolerate such a thwarting of his handi-
work? God remained faithful to what he had begun, and he
intervened with a powerful hand. It is that same powerful
hand that, even nowadays, is the inspiration and the hope of
any liberation theology.

Afterwards, when the difference between rich and
poor had begun to divide the Israelite nation itself, prophets
rose to protest against this development in the name of the
very same God. They did it in a language that left no doubt
about God's intentions. They spoke about God's pity for the
poor and the oppressed. They shouted his indignation toward
the rich who had much more than they needed, and who
refused to share with others who did not have enough to live
on. They lamented, in the name of God, about the sabo-
taging of the God-given life-dynamism.

Isaiah warned them that all their religious practices,
their fasting and their prayers would remain unheard, unseen
and useless. He shouted that God had never asked for
fasting, but that he had asked them to share their food with
the hungry, their home with the roofless and their clothing
with the naked. He said that God had asked them not to run
away from their own flesh and blood, from their fellow
human beings in need.

Jeremiah repeated the same complaints. He did it in
another way. He warned them not to content themselves by
saying (Jeremiah 7:4-7):

We are safe! This is the Lord's temple, this is the
Lord's temple, this is the Lord's temple! You put
your trust in deceitful words. Change the way you
are living and stop doing the things you are doing.
Be fair in your treatment of one another. Stop tak-

ing advantage of aliens, orphans, and widows. Stop killing innocent people in this land. Stop worshipping other gods, for that will destroy you!

In this special preference for the oppressed, God tried, according to the words of those prophets, to restore balance. God remained interested in the life of *all*.

The Commandments as Life Codes

The same interest, or care, for the oppressed is shown in the formulation of a command of God that was especially dear to the Hebrews: to have one holiday a week, the seventh day, as the Sabbath.

That day has something to do with God's creative work. It is the day that God started to rest after his labor in power and might. God, of course, did not need that rest. The description of God's resting is given to lend a divine motivation to something that is very important for the life God created.

The repose was prescribed for several reasons. The one best known to us is to be free for a day to praise and thank our Creator. There is also another reason. We are not allowed to work in order to give ourselves the rest we need. Even this does not seem to be the last reason.

There is a third one. The free day was also ordered to guarantee a day of rest to the servant, the maid, to the slaves, and even to the domesticated animals in the homesteads. Leisure is necessary for human life. It is during leisure that many of our best ideas are born. It is at rest when visions arise. Without such a holiday there would be no survival. The world would perish while working endlessly. Even in the most harsh concentration camps of Germany and Russia, one day of rest a week was kept.

This biblical prescription is a kind of survival code. The Book of Deuteronomy tells us that all the laws of God should be seen in this light. Those laws and commandments are given to make human life possible. Preachers often say, with the best of intentions, we will be rewarded with longevity when we keep the commandments, when we, e.g., honor our fathers and our mothers. There is more to the keeping of those laws than just gaining a reward.

The laws are absolutely essential for human life. If we don't keep them, we will perish. Human life, and life in general, would simply be impossible.

Those laws and regulations are given with human life itself. They were given to us in another manner than to the infrahuman creatures. Plants and animals come into life with their programming practically built in. The human being has to work out his or her program in community. A code of law, such as the Hebrews developed in their ten commandments, has to be taken into account in that organization of our programming.

No human society can permit theft in its midst. Without the law, all human relations would be troubled and incapacitated. No human community would be able to allow murder without itself being killed. No group of human beings would be able to survive total sexual promiscuity.

These codes and commandments are conditions without which human survival would be impossible. They should not be restricted to the famous ten. We already heard of how Isaiah tried to explain that the differences between the rich and the poor are a threat to society, too. He understood that when those inequalities grew (as they are doing all over the world today), our human life, with all its facets, would be endangered.

In all those commandments and prohibitions, the Old Testament's authors pointed to God's caring for human life. It is that care, that option of God for human life, which had to be the center of Hebrew worship. It should be the center of the lives of all who live from within that tradition. It is the center of Jesus' existence among us today.

3

Anti-Creationism

Not so very long ago, a small single-engined plane crashed in one of the most deserted rain forests in Brazil. The pilot died in the crash. The only passenger remained uninjured. He was found a few miles from the plane. He had not a single wound, and most probably he had been able to escape from the plane without difficulty.

When the rescue team found him, he was dead. He definitely did not die of starvation, loss of blood or anything like that. He most probably died of fear. It was the only explanation one could think of. Crashed into the dark of a forest, totally alien to him, he had not had sufficient time to get accustomed to the noises, movements and smells around him. He had not been able to "place" them; he had not been able to explain them. Consequently, he died of fear.

In March 1975 a bomb exploded in a bus in Nairobi. The bus was just about ready to leave for upcountry and was filled with people going home. The explosion was not a terribly heavy one, but about twenty-five people died in the blast, most of them farmers from the neighborhood. Many of those who died were not wounded. The doctors explained that they had died of shock. Some of them were killed running in panic against the walls of houses near the bus stop. They died because they had not been able to understand quickly enough what had happened and that they had not been hurt.

Every human being, and every community needs an explanation of what is going on it its environment. The need to understand what is going on around us is related to our survival. We need explanations; otherwise, we would die of fear.

Even animals seem to have that need. A cat in a strange house will be afraid and hide until it can "explain" all the noises of its new home. At the moment that it can "place" all those noises, it will come out of its hiding, its fear over.

Anyone who sleeps in a strange room and wakes up during the night hearing an odd noise will not be able to fall asleep again until that noise is explained. He will get out of bed to check. If he finds out that the noise was caused by a tree branch squeaking next to the open window, the sound is cleared and he will be able to go back to sleep. Without such an explanation, he would have remained awake, waiting for the first light of day.

One of the first reasons why human beings began scientific research must have been that necessity to overcome or to prevent those fears and anxieties. Without those explanations human life would have been impossible in the long run.

There were, of course, other reasons to motivate that quest for knowledge and insight. We are curious, too. Not only do we want to explain what is happening in the present. We hope to be able to understand the behavior of things around us, in order to control them in the future. We would like to know what is going to happen.

The most fundamental motive, however, is fear, which implies that in our scientific research human life is the center of interest. In order to be able to survive, we have built our theories; in order to increase that life quantitatively and qualitatively, we have given birth to atoms and spirits, to numbers and laws.

Our original knowledge implied faith in the value and the importance of human life. Our life is our reality. Every opinion overlooking that fact is dangerous for life. Every belief that deviates from that faith in life is idolatrous, superstitious and *anti-creational*.

Things and Persons/Atoms and Spirits

Though we need to understand our environment (and ourselves) to be able to survive, there is much we cannot directly explain or understand. Even the material world remains to a great extent a total mystery to us. We are never able to dive into the real depth of our beings. We face innumerable mysteries and riddles. Most probably, that is good.

Whenever science progresses, we are led to serious ethical complications. As we delve into genetic engineering, the question arises: Is it ethically wise to apply our knowledge? We are able to do all kinds of things, and every day our research reveals more of them, but should we be allowed to do them?

That question is more urgent, as we really do not have a direct insight into life or into the reality around us. We know them only by way of our thinking models.

A good (and old) example is our classical and antiquated atom theory. We did not understand matter around us. We had no direct access to it. One specific part of matter intrigued us in a very special way. It seemed to have all kinds of magical properties. Iron moved, expanded, shrank, could get very hot and liquify, and so on. Because Western scientists did not understand its behavior, they supposed that iron and all matter is composed of small particles, atoms. The idea was not new. Greek philosophers and scientists used that thinking model long before the birth of Jesus Christ.

With the help of that "thing" thinking, many ideas became explicable and understandable to the extent that many people began to believe that atoms form the substance of all matter. They began to believe that those atoms, which they had thought out for themselves, existed in reality.

Because of the success of that explanation, or more accurately, of that supposition, everything started to pivot around things in the most literal sense of the word. Human life began to pivot around things. In no time people started to consider themselves as things.

When a sick person goes to a doctor he is not surprised that the doctor regards him as an enormous molecule. If a person is sick, there must be something wrong with his physical or chemical composition, so some "thing" has to be added or removed.

Historians and psychologists developed theories in which they maintained that one finds in human society the same deterministic laws as in the world of matter.

Even in religious matters one gave into that thing-adoration. Grace became a reality to be added and subtracted, increased and diminished, measured and weighed. Enormous and very beautiful churches and cathedrals were built. And notwithstanding our growing insight, those things (even cathedrals are things), did not help very much, religious communities kept on building them.

The old lessons from the prophets had been forgotten. Jeremiah and Amos would wring their hands in many of our modern religious constructions. They would shout again that salvation cannot be found in things.

Societies throughout the world had to deal with the same problems. They had to explain their environment with its sounds and developments, its colors and smells, its sun, moon, tides, deserts, volcanic eruptions, thunderstorms and earthquakes, and "life" in a piece of iron.

The African society had no direct access to the reality they were standing in either. They, too, had to use thinking models. In as far as we can see, the thinkers in practically the whole of Africa used another model. They said, "Let us proceed as if matter were composed of personified powers and forces: spirits."[2]

Through this model they were able to explain their reality. Fear must have been taken away. In Africa, too, the success of their thinking model became so enchanting that they started to believe that those "spirits" formed the substance of reality. They began to think that what originally was only imagined by them could explain the world around and was reality itself.

Why That Difference?

Why were things chosen to explain reality in Western culture and personified powers and forces chosen in Africa (and most probably also in the pre-western West and North)?

The discussion around that problem is old, at least as old as the study by Sir James Frazer in *The Golden Bough*.[3] The most acceptable answer to this issue is to be found in the historical backgrounds of the two models. The Greeks, who first thought of the atomic model, lived in towns. The spirit model derives from a non-urban setting.

When Africans started to look for a model to explain nature, they chose the most regular pattern they could think of, found in their well-organized interhuman relationships. Those relations were fixed from birth to death, and even after. Africa trusted people more than things.

In the urbanized environment of the Greek towns, those relations had broken down, much as they do in practically all town centers. Looking for a regular behavior pattern, human behavior did not qualify. They trusted things more than people.

In Africa one opted for life, not for things. It is humanity that African society chose to further in cooperation with God's creational impulse. It seems that this choice is the heritage they lived with from the very beginning. It is a heritage that forcefully strikes every visitor to Africa. It is a way of thinking and being from which we Westerners can learn.

When we chose the thing model to explain reality, we chose our preference for objects, things that are made, that are finished. It seems difficult to explain life in that thing-way. As the great American philosopher, William James, noted long ago:

> When from our present advanced standpoint, we look back upon past stages of human thought, we are amazed that a universe which appears to us so vast and mysterious a complication should ever have seemed to anyone so little and plain a *thing*.

There is nothing in the spirit and principles of science that need hinder science from dealing successfully with a world in which personal forces are the starting point of new effects.[4]

The Gospel and Things

There is a story about things in the Gospel. It is a parable attributed to Jesus. It is the story of a coat. The coat, or cloak, was very old. It had a hole in it. The owner was so attached to that old piece of clothing, or maybe it was his only cover, that he decided to have it repaired. He bought a new piece of cloth, shiny and unshrunk. He sewed that new piece of material over the hole in the old coat.

Once the coat was repaired, he washed it. He splashed it in water, rubbed it with soap, and put the wet coat over a washing line to dry in the sun. As the new patch began to dry, being in the sun and water for the first time, it shrank. It shrank a great deal. But the old coat did not shrink. Old as it was, it could not shrink any more.

When the coat was dry, the owner put it on. It tore again around the newly attached piece of cloth. The new tear was larger and more conspicuous than the old tear.

Things do not live. Things cannot adapt.

There is another story with the same lesson. This time it is about an old winesack. The sack was made of leather. The leather of that bag was so old that it had lost all its elasticity. It was stiff and rigid. The young wine poured into it by mistake was full of life and power. It was bubbling and fermenting. It was "alive." The old sack could not handle that young life. It burst open, and all the wine was lost in the sand.

The coat was a thing, the winesack was a thing. Things are rigid. If you force a thing, it breaks, or cracks, or splits. Things have little or no elasticity.

Is that not our complaint about bureaucracy, the rule of the desk and computer, papers, files, numbers, documents, or statistics?

St. Paul rejects that thing thinking radically when reflecting upon the effects of his preaching. He wrote that God had not grafted the new, life-giving Spirit onto things, stone tablets, or slates, but into living hearts. Hearts open to growth.

Anti-Creational Superstition

Americans and Europeans are very often of the opinion that Africans are superstitious. Is not the African traditional world populated with all kinds of spirits and other spooky beings? Under the influence of those Americans and Europeans, and especially of the missionaries who came to preach among them, Africans began to believe themselves to be superstitious.

They often are. In a country like Kenya, where the local press has the liberty to speak rather openly about anything they want, that superstition is obvious when you read the papers.

After the 1983 elections a number of candidates for Parliament filed petitions against the result of those elections because they accused the successful candidates of having used magic in their campaigns. They had sprinkled the electorate with "holy" water, or they had made them swear oaths in rather sinister ceremonies.

Not so long ago the coach of a Kenyan football team dismissed a couple of players because they refused to listen to him and remained playing according to the "instructions" obtained from the intestines of a ceremonially sacrificed hen.

Africans are, however, not superstitious because they have populated their world with spirits and personified powers. They did that to develop sufficient thinking models to overcome their fear and to get some control over their environment.

Africans became superstitious at the moment they were overruled by their own thought-out, or even to a certain extent, imagined thinking models. It was at that point that they lost themselves, and no longer considered human life as all-important and the center of everything. It is at that juncture that they lost faith in the power of their own, real human life.

They began to dance and to sing, to bless and to curse around something else. They started to sacrifice human life to those spirits and powers. Their faith, turned into superstition, became very dangerous.

There are fewer reflections by Africans about Americans and Europeans but some do exist. Africans talked about those people from the West around their evening fires from the moment these intruders entered their continent. Up until recently those conversations have never been registered. Now they are. Africans, of course, often seem to think about the white people in much the way we think about them.

To give a rather humorous example in another field of interest: American and European tourists like to rent mini-buses in Nairobi to take pictures of the natives from the roof-tops of those specially adapted cars, a rather unpleasant habit from the African point of view. They do not like to be filmed or photographed as curiosities. The Maasai especially have difficulties in tolerating this involuntary exposure. Yet, as they live rather near Nairobi (in fact, Nairobi is a Maasai word), they are often the victims.

A couple of Maasai students, sick of being so filmed, rented their own mini-bus in town. They got some film and a camera. Every time they saw a group of Americans or Europeans stop for a picnic on a roadside or gaze at some local sight, they would stop their bus and begin to film them, to the great consternation of those visitors. They did this while dressed in their traditional brick-red robes, with all the customary niceties: spears, beads, ear ornaments. Let us return to our subject.

Many Africans consider the white people to be very superstitious. It is no exaggeration to say that many older Africans consider the Westerners to be nothing but great children. According to them, the whites have their world populated with so many things that they have lost sight of human life itself because of all those gadgets. According to Africans, the Westerners' judgments are based on the value of things rather than on the value of human life.

A typical example is time. Time is "worshipped" by Americans and Europeans alike. They are known as people of the clock. For them, ten o'clock is ten o'clock. When one makes an appointment for ten, one should be at that appointment at ten. In this way time, nicely and pragmatically measured, starts to reign over humanity, submitting us to its powers.

First, time, the space in which our human relations grow, essentially something very social, was made into a thing.

Second, this thing was fixed to towers and walls. Later, it even became attached to the wrists of practically everyone, checking the lives in all those pulses and regulating them. Time, a thing, became more important than life. This is not (yet) true of all human societies.

There is a meeting somewhere in East Africa of school heads and some notables. One European is present. The meeting should have started at ten o'clock. It is already much later. The man from the West is looking at his watch from time to time. He does it rather furtively, but still, it is noticed. One in the company says, "Who chose the time?" The answer comes without any further complication: "We did." The point being: why should we then be bothered if we don't keep to that time? Aren't we in charge of our time?

The answer to that last question in America and Europe is: No. Time, the work program, the moon, the sun, the atom, money, production time, our appointment diary, and agenda are in charge of us.

Things become the center of our lives. Life suffers because of them. Life perishes. Humanity dances around one of its mental figments and forgets about itself in that superstitious worship.

We, people from the West, are superstitious in the eyes of many Africans, because we believe in things. We sacrifice our lives, our hearts, our stomachs and all we have and are to those things.

An old man sitting somewhere under a tree alongside a busy road once said to me in the dark of a falling evening, pointing at the headlights of the oncoming cars, "Do you see those lights? They are the eyes of unborn, sacrificed children.

Every car could have been a child or two in that family. They choose cars instead of children.'' A rather simplified way of reasoning, and yet . . . .

A difference existed between the superstition in Africa and the West. In Africa one concentrated oneself on life and life-relations. In the West, "things" got the upper hand over life. Life often became something artificial, something synthetic. In each case, however, human life was threatened, especially at the moment when the two cultures started to contact each other.

Another type of idolatry and superstition should be mentioned. It is a belief again by which a reality, different from human life, is placed in the center of one's attention. It is a superstition often called fascism. As soon as a group considers itself as the center of the world, superior to others, another human figment of the imagination is turned into reality.

A group that sets itself apart from all the others, despising those who are not part of it, is idolatrous, and definitely anti-creationist. This kind of apartheid, an idea the prophets protested against throughout the Bible, contradicts the reality of life as it was created. It prefers a part to the whole. It is a kind of cancer. It does not correspond to God's intention as described in the Bible. It does not even accept the very first human story in the Bible, the one about Adam and Eve.

The Relevance of the Old Testament's Stories

Europeans often do not realize that they are superstitious. We do not mean the revival of the Western belief in devils, witches, and evil spirits. Although that revival is spectacular, and very much stimulated by a corresponding film industry, it remains, nevertheless, in the margin and in the fringe of Western life.

We mean the kind of superstition that seems to determine the center of Western culture itself. It is our own thinking models, our technology, and science in general, that prevail over anything else.

No one will defend that position in theory. No one will ever make that choice in public. In the practice of everyday life, however, that option is demonstrated every time the appointment book, the system, or bureaucracy are preferred to ourselves, our wives, our children, and to human life in general.

Somewhere in Holland a new hospital had to be built in a middle-sized municipality. The trustees were Catholics. At the laying of the cornerstone, the local parish priest said that the project was so prestigious that its construction might result in at least two heart attacks. Not a nice thing to say, and he did not say it in public. He was right. His prophecy was fulfilled before the construction was completed.

It is, of course, nonsense to speak in such a context of human sacrifices. It would be crazy to compare those deaths with the offering of young men on the old sacrificial offering stones among the Aztecs in South America in honor of the sun. But is it?

Where is the leader, the religious leader, the prophet who can help us to escape from a system where those types of sacrifices are brought without any further fuss, though we all know about them? Where will we find the guide who is to lead us out of the Egypt where we are caught and where the managers of the system want to double our production, insisting that our children should not be born?

Who will be able to convince us to leave the fleshpots of that Egypt behind, together with all the things we have collected here, in view of a new destination and a new country? We have plenty of theologians; our religions are famous for their theologians. Where are the prophets?

It is a pity that we started to call the Old Testament old, and that most of us only know it in the form of a set of pious tales for children and adults. We cannot even understand Jesus if we do not know the Bible, his Holy Book. The Old Testament was the Bible of Jesus. Without that book he would have been unable to become rooted in the history of humanity.

The reasons why many people disregard the Bible are not difficult to trace. The Bible expresses that God gave Hebrews of that time an insight into what was happening around them. Though religious in its intention, his word

seemed also to give a factual explanation. Modern science —
anthropology, sociology and history included — have often
found the Bible faulty in its factual content. Most intelligent
people are, by now, aware of the difficulties of accepting as
fact such stories as the creation of *one* human couple, the
paradise situation, the great flood, and even some of the
Israelite military successes. For many, the whole of the
Bible's content lost value because of these critical observa-
tions which, as such, had little to do with the real intent of the
divinely inspired authors.

Disregarding the Bible means doing away with all its
stories. Without those stories our whole original Western
Christian attitude falls away. We will no longer have stories
about how life began. We will no longer have stories about
life's end, either. Our lives become meaningless, untold.

The old pagan stories and legends became lost over a
thousand years ago under the influence of that very same
Bible.

In Jesus we were grafted onto the old Judaic root, the
old Jewish tradition. Now if that root, that trunk falls away,
the only thing left is our modern science. Science alone knows
nothing about our beginning, about our meaning and about
our destiny. Science will never be able to tell the stories our
children are looking for when they ask, "Where do we come
from, what are we heading for?"

Children will continue to ask those questions. Those
children's questions are the most important ones we have.
Those queries are among our most precious treasures. They
are coming from the deepest well within us. Jesus of
Nazareth, when he was a child of twelve, remained behind in
the temple to be able to continue to ask questions. And, as a
grown man, he told the crowd if they didn't become like
children, they wouldn't be able to enter the Kingdom of God.

Our children's questions are answered in the Bible. Its
stories are meant to be symbolic answers to those questions.
The stories often contain serious warnings directed against
those who, as the biblical texts solemnly declare, make "the
works of their hands and minds" the center of their lives, and
kneel in front of them. The warnings are directed to those

who even go so far as to sacrifice their own children, the fruits of their own loins and wombs, to their idols, and thus block the creational impulse in themselves.

The central message of the Old Testament is a warning against that anti-creational, sacrificial custom. It is the most serious and repeated complaint of the prophets.

Those warnings, too, disappeared, together with turning from the Bible. And even if we have kept telling those stories, if we are still reading them, few of us are convinced that those old sacrificial tales have any significance for our days. They seem to be a part of a long lost and forgotten past.

Nevertheless, that hospital in Holland had to be built, and it was going to be built in a way that would cost the lives of two people.

And that friend of yours who recently died of a sudden heart attack had his calendar fully booked until about three weeks after his death. Yet, they later said that he had felt tired the last days of his life. Why had he not taken time to rest?

How often are we put before that kind of choice ourselves? It is at these moments that we should remember those stories in the Bible, those prophetic warnings. The Old Testament remains relevant. For many, intolerably so.

Part II

JESUS
and
CREATION

4

Jesus and Creation

The astrologers who came from the East, according to St. Matthew's report, are generally called wise men. Tradition tells us that there were three of them. St. Matthew does not write so, but as the visitors offered three gifts, they are supposed to have been three men. In most modern and critical studies of the New Testament, the men are considered to be legendary people, who most probably never actually traveled the roads to Bethlehem. Thus they are characters in what might be called a fairytale as they appear before the child, Jesus.

In such an explanation they are mythical human beings. They are part of an interpretation, a bit of theology. That is a pity. Theology is only theory, and any human being is more important than a theory. In the Gospel of Matthew, the story is about living human beings. A story full of people is more important than any theory. Even the great theological theoretician, Edward Schillebeeckx, writes at the end of his massive work on Jesus that the whole of his theology would mean nothing if it would not lead to a faith in which the stories are told.[5] The subtitle of his book on Jesus is *The Story of Someone Alive.*

The story of those three wise men is a good example of a *living* story. They had seen a bright star, in itself rather common. But at the same time they had seen something else through, and behind that star.

Something new was in the offing. It was like a warning

before a totally new development. Something like a new order, a change-over, or salvation, was hanging in the air. Something was new between heaven and earth. It was not something static or fixed. It was moving and developing. It was "alive." And the three—whether they came from the same place or from three different directions does not matter very much—decided to follow that movement. They packed their things and left their countries, families, and belongings to follow the star.

Then the star stopped somewhere around Jerusalem. By that time the men had already made up their minds as to what they were looking for. The newness, the liberation or salvation was according to them not to be found in the town archives. They were not looking for a theory, a new psychological trend, a modern educational method or a laboratory. Don't forget: they were wise! They were looking for *someone*, they were asking: "Where is that child?" They were asking for a new king. In their wisdom, they knew that if a real answer to their quest was available, it could be only in the form of a person, of a new human being.

Those wise men must have been traveling because of an insight, a wisdom they possessed before they even started their safari. Their attitude implies, at the same time, that they considered their own situation as temporary and provisional. Their visions were not closed. They were open to newness. That openness and wisdom must have been based on intuition, a religious second sight.

The Book of Deuteronomy tells us of how God gave each nation its heritage from the moment humanity was divided over the whole of the earth (Deuteronomy 32:8). Those wise men must have been influenced by their part of that heritage, when the light of the new star suddenly burst through the ceiling of the world into their lives.

Looking for a Child

There must have been a reason why those magi were on the look-out for a new life-impulse. Why did they start their search? We are accustomed to answering this question by referring to such terms as redemption, liberation from sin, and salvation. We learned that Jesus came to save us from our sins. We are so used to that idea that most probably it would never occur to us that other groups of human beings might base their search for new life differently.

The fact, however, that the Western idea of sin is not to be found all over the world might make us reconsider. In certain European religious traditions one knows not only that those wise men were three; one even knows their three names: Caspar, Melchior, and Balthasar, and from where they came. In parts of the southern Lowlands and German Rhineland children dress up at the occasion of Epiphany. One will be an Indian, another a Chinese, and the third, most imposing, an African. The peoples they represent built, with their original heritage, rather different world visions. Of course, it is impossible to dwell on those ideas in the context of this book. A few very simplifying remarks will have to suffice.

The Hindu, whose name derives from the Indus, the river after which India was named, has one great desire: to flow back into the divine Godhead from which he flows forth. That urge should not even be called a desire. According to the Hindu, one should have no desire at all, but to return simply to the cosmic totality. Each drop of water belongs to the ocean.

Traditionally the Chinese has a totally different ideal. He tries to live in harmony with himself. He tries to realize, as well as possible, his TAO, a kind of life-law, a personal blueprint without too much external fuss or ostentation. He wants to live as simply and naturally as possible.

His life-model is the element water. Water never starts to move by itself; it always flows to the lowest place and stays there. Yet, it can develop a terrific force if it meets resistance.

What the African astrologer came to look for in Bethlehem is more difficult to explain. Up to very recently, the African world vision was not taken very seriously. The thought that Africa would be able to teach us something about religion or anything else is very new. The possibility was expressed for the first time in Placide Tempels's book, *Bantu Philosophy*, published in 1943 in Antwerp, Belgium.[6]

At the moment, African scholars and others seem to agree that the world vision of the African in general is a kind of humanism. The center of interest, also of the religious interest, is human life, seen in relationship to its total environment. The first issue is survival, but it is not only a question of food, drink, and shelter. Those who died and those who are as yet unborn belong to life, too. Life is given not only to be lived merely in a minimum survival pattern. Life should be celebrated! It should be danced! God the creator and giver of life can be honored and praised only by its celebration.

Let us come back to our question. What were those wise men looking for in Bethlehem?

It is not even easy to define what Jesus' Jewish contemporaries expected from him. Most of them seemingly expected a purely political liberation from a foreign yoke. Though the Old Testament had been rather clear on the point, it seems that practically no one realized at the time of his death on the cross that he died for the sins of all. This idea and interpretation would only grow afterwards.

Maybe it is an unusual question, but what did our own ancestors hope to achieve when they decided to turn to Christ? It is difficult to guess at their motives almost one and a half thousand years later. Had Clovis the sense of sin with which our theologians worked?

Some time ago an article in a Tanzania newspaper caused some furor. A theologizing journalist wrote that the concept of original sin was nothing but a Western import. The three who arrived at Bethlehem after Jesus' birth probably did not think about sin in those terms either. They came with different expectations and other questions, if we really would like to see them as typical representatives of their traditional backgrounds.

The African in that legendary group must have had his own anticipations too, expectations which, as such, had little to do with our classical idea of sin. He wanted to live, live to the full. It is that type of life for which he came to look. It is that type of life Jesus promised him when he said, "I came to bring life, life to the full!"

Many theologians, the great and the less great ones,

often express their worry about the concept of sin, or rather what our idea of it has become. Salvation, theologians are accustomed to think, is difficult if those to be saved have no sense of sin. Pope John Paul II told his community in April 1983 that the loss of the sense of sin was "the most frightening of all evils which afflict the world today." In his theology it means that humanity no longer needs Jesus.

It seems that in most of Western theology Jesus and the concept of salvation from sin are so intimately connected that one does not make sense without the other. No sin, no Jesus. Was that not the reason some mystics said without hesitation, "Felix culpa! Happy guilt!," as if they wanted to say, "Fortunately we sinned; otherwise, Jesus would never have come."

Is that necessarily so? Even in the high time of this kind of medieval Christian theology another question remained: Would Christ have come if humanity had not sinned? Thomas Aquinas thought not, but his Franciscan contemporaries contradicted him on that point. They thought that Jesus would have come even if humanity had not fallen away from its original state. There is no doubt: the relation between the coming of Jesus and sin has always been stressed in Judaeo-Christian experience.

It is not our intention to deny this relationship, or to do away with the fall. One question, however, which one cannot answer in this manner, is what to do with those numbers of our human family who never developed such an idea of sin simply because they did not know about its reality? If someone has no knowledge of this type of sin, he cannot be interested in Jesus because of it.

Would there be other motives possible, leading to the importance of Jesus? Would there be other motives, implying in another sense what we call sin or sins? Is there the possibility of complementary interpretations regarding the salvation, liberation, and redemption Jesus brought?

Again, what were those three wise men looking for in Bethlehem? What was the African wise man looking for? What are the Africans nowadays looking for when they, in their turn, travel to seek Jesus?

Looking for Life

We already described the African world vision in a few sentences. In this vision an attempt is made to relate to one's environment in such a way that life will quantitatively and qualitatively increase in community. This attitude situates the African in another way in his world than his Western, or from the African point of view, his Northern, contemporary. The African is more directly interested in life, and especially in human life. The conviction that life should be continued, and that one should survive in one's children, seems to a great extent to have disappeared in the West. The direct bond to the earth, the necessity to coax the earth to render food and water, is practically fallen away in our regions. That kind of work is done elsewhere, very often in the Third World.

When a tourist from Europe was told in Kenya that there was hardly any food left in the northern regions of that country because of a continuous drought, she asked, "Are there no shops there?" as if shops produce the food. In a sense she was right. The shops had provided food throughout her life. In her case hunger would have meant nothing but an empty shop. In Africa hunger means an empty field, a burnt forest, a dry river or a silted well.

In one way or another, life in America and Europe became alienated from reality. In the Third World life is more directly lived. Life there is blood and sweat, ploughing, and the fetching of water that is sometimes hours and hours away, day in and day out. Survival, the growing and producing of food and drink in such an environment, cannot be something left to one individual, not even to an individualized nuclear family. It can be done only in community, in an extended family, within a clan context.

This community, the family, and the clan came first. The individual came second. The activities developed were definitely personal, but hardly individual. The whole of life was directed toward the welfare of the community. One's personal welfare depended totally on the welfare of the common welfare. Even the most personal transitions in the development of human life, such as birth, puberty, marriage, sickness, and death were communally organized. The individual could not imagine survival outside his community. It is rather obvious that in such a context the concept of salvation and even sin are different from what they are in a Western frame of reference.

The Western missionary came (and comes) with a message of salvation of each personal soul, a reality hardly functioning in African thought. Africans wanted, in the first place, to be liberated from their daily worries. They wanted to be saved from the whims of an unreliable weather pattern or from their fear of wild animals and poisonous snakes; they wanted to be liberated from sickness and premature death, from existing inequalities and all sorts of disasters.

They wanted children, many children, and especially many sons. They wanted to be protected against spirits, witches, magic, and the possible bad influences of the deceased or, as yet, unborn members of their families.

Added to all this should be the great desire, a more personal desire, to be able to continue to work for the welfare of the group to which one belonged. Those aspirations have, of course, something to do with "good" and "evil." Evil, however, presents itself differently from its interpretation in the Western Judaeo-Christian tradition. To give an example, in some African communities a girl who masturbates is calling up an evil power, causing harm not only to herself, but to the whole of the community. Because of that harm she and her entire community are to undergo a purification rite. God has nothing to do with all this. A sense of sin in which God is offended by our misdeeds often seems not to be developed.

In Western Christianity one would accept, too, that evil has an influence in the whole of the community. In African tradition, evil is seen as something that kills human society. An act is bad because it hinders the healthy development and outgrowth of that society. We can say this in more of a theological sense: an act is bad, because it opposes the continuation of creation.

Continuation of Creation

This vision entails a search for possibilities in view of a further outgrowth in the ever changing environment. One wanted to be liberated from sickness and from all forms of "possession."

Most independent African churches (those that split off from the imported mission churches) concentrate themselves in their worship on those types of issues: healing and the chasing out of evil spirits and devils. They do this to enable everyone to cooperate in what God started among us through creation.

Jesus Christ said, "I have come to bring life, life to the full!" From the moment the Africans heard and believed this, they jumped up, looking for their drums, their tambourines, their string instruments, their flutes and their rattling *kayambas* and *calebases* to accompany their alleluias to praise the Lord. To be a Christian there is different from being a Christian elsewhere.

The Psychology of Conversion

The number of people in Africa who join Jesus Christ in his triumphant victory in this world is enormous. The statistician David Barrett, author of the *World Christian Encyclopedia*,[7] wrote an article in 1970 in which he projected 350 million Christians in Africa by the year 2000.[8]

In 1980 he had to correct that prognosis in an interview with *Time* magazine. His projection had not been too high, as is usually the case. It had been too low. By the year 2000 most probably there will be more than 500 million Christians in Africa, the average daily number of baptisms being 16 thousand. In a way, things seem to go so easily that the tendency exists to be a bit suspicious of all this. Even the newly baptized are sometimes worried. They ask themselves the question: "How was it possible that we gave in so easily?" Other questions are beginning to be asked: "How is it that we left our old customs behind us so quickly? Why do we no longer attach value to our own older religious traditions?"

If one ever tried to answer those questions, it was done in Western theological and pastoral terms. The research was generally done by missionaries. Only very recently have Africans started to answer those queries which are the more interesting and, in a sense, more alarming because the research done shows more and more that the older traditional organizational forms were far from naive or primitive. They were very effective and show a high degree of sophistication. They allowed for human life in sometimes extremely grim circumstances. Why was all this left behind; why was all this declared invalid and old fashioned?

It is, of course, the Africans who should answer these questions and they have started to do that.[9] The results of that African research often upset the European missionaries who are, in certain cases, even deeply offended. A Catholic priest from Kenya wrote a 250-page dissertation on the work of the missionaries and catechists in his region. In the first version of that study, the name Jesus Christ had not been mentioned once!

The study was on his own people, the Gikuyus, a very important group of people in Kenya, numbering about three to four million. He made it clear that the motives for which the Gikuyus became Christians did not at all correspond to the ideals of the missionaries. Those missionaries had come to save souls.

They did this by preaching the death and resurrection of Jesus Christ on the cross, by the celebration of Baptism and the other sacraments. They wanted to save the Gikuyus from hell. Having no idea of hell, and having absolutely no doubt about the continuation of life after death, this issue caused no problem among their converts. They did not need that type of salvation. They were interested in something else.

They were very impressed by the enormous power and vitality of the missionaries. They were overwhelmed by the European way of life. They wanted to adapt as soon as possible to this totally new kind of environment. To them those white people came from another planet. They wanted to survive this invasion, which by the way had been prophesized by some of their traditional prophets. The Africans wanted to participate in this new life; they wanted to be initiated into it as soon as possible.

The churches with their schools and hospitals seemed to offer this initiation and survival possibility. By accepting them, life would remain possible, and it would be qualitatively improved, if not changed completely.

The *Word* by which and in which they had been created, according to those missionaries, would help them on, if only to clarify all kinds of remaining confusions in religion and life.

The Africans were, however, not interested in theoretical questions in the first place. They were interested in the person, Jesus. They experienced him as a giver of new life, the giver of a new relationship to God, their creator.

Life is in the final instance always *someone*, the new child those three wise men in the beginning of this chapter were looking for. Creation is continued in life only.

5

Jesus' Creative Words: Abba and Amen

Every time God opened his mouth in those first stories of creation, part of the world or life came into existence or was changed. God said: air; and the winds began to howl with pleasure. God said: earth; and that earth has not stopped settling since. God said: animals; and birds began to whistle, the fish never stopped swimming, and all kinds of animals started to mate, reproducing the joy of their lives. God said: Adam; and he looked up. God said: Eve; and she stood next to Adam, looking more at Adam than at God. God said: multply; and from then on children were conceived and born. God said: be stewards over nature; and the people began to change the world within, and around them, to further God's creative dynamism in them.

God did not stop speaking. God sent his word to Moses and the prophets, to the judges and the kings, to the priests and the lawmakers. In the end God sent Jesus. Jesus did not come just like that. He came at the moment when the earth and the world were ready for him. He came when humanity had reached a certain degree of maturity in its evolution. He came at the point when it would have been impossible to go on without him.

He came, as we have good reasons to believe, when humanity had been living for a few million years, developing

and growing through all sorts of adventures, transitions, con-
flicts, cultures, inventions, and events, all the time pressurized
by an enormous creational dynamism. That humanity slowly
became more self-reliant and more free.

When Jesus entered the world he was "carried" and
"upheld" by all those people who went before him. He was
not born in isolation, and he should not be perceived in isolation either. He grew forth from the life of his people, a new
sprout on a very old branch. He should be seen in the light of
the experience and expectations of his people. He should be
seen in the light of the visions of all prophets and seers before
him. He stood, so to speak, on the shoulders of all those who
had preceded him in their misery and joy, in their sorrow and
happiness. He was bound to that past, connected to the
human heritage of all the preceding generations.

We say that he came to take away our sins. Our concept of sin was expressed by Jesus and by those who left their
descriptions of him to us and who interpreted his death and
resurrection in a peculiar way. When Jesus spoke about what
we now call sin, he used the expressions: the missing of the
mark, not living up to standard, remaining below expectations. When he said, "I came to save sinners," he said, "I
came for those who are missing the mark." Sinners were the
"missers" of the mark.

To Jesus, sin did not seem to be something on its own.
It was not a blemish or an offense. It was not even a missed
chance. It was an act not up to what one might expect from a
human being. It was an attitude beneath the old standard,
and definitely far under the new standard Jesus introduced.
With the development of human life, the standard had been
growing, too. In Jesus' time one could expect more of a human
community than in the time of the beginning of humanity.

Even if someone would realize completely, and
without fail, the older human standard of life, he would have
fallen short of what had become possible in the new order of
human existence.

Jesus himself said so when he remarked that John the
Baptist, though the greatest one in the old order, was in fact

lesser than anyone in the new order. John was the glorious fulfillment of the Old Testament, and at the same time the beginning of the new one. John knew this and stated: "I am not even worthy to bind the straps of Jesus' sandals."

Jesus not only came to help the old "missers" to hit their aim. He came to introduce a new destiny, a new norm and a new standard. He came to give life; he came to give *his* life. He came in the context of the creation story. The beginning of the gospel by John is full of references to creation. Standing on the past, Jesus came to open a new chapter in the history of humanity, a fresh and more vigorous blow of breath and spirit from our Creator.

Jesus' Creative Word: Abba

God's creative words turned the nothingness and chaos of the beginning into an ordered and "good" world. Jesus, expressing God's word, spoke too. Jesus spoke above and amid the chaos of human existence. His words placed the whole of creation in a new perspective. He did that, theologians tell us, in one or two words. They are the only words, according to the exegetes, that can be attributed to Jesus, himself: *Ipsissima verba.* The words have come down to us just as he had spoken them, words of the Bible that even nowadays remain untranslated in most editions. Those two words are Abba and Amen.

Though the Aramaic word *Abba* is quoted only once in the Greek Gospels (Mark 14:36), exegetes such as Schillebeeckx, Jeremias, and van Iersel are convinced that Jesus used the word habitually, and that it should be heard whenever the words "Father," "the Father," "my Father," "your Father," or even "their Father," are used by him. It was also the word he must have used, according to the same exegetes, when he taught his disciples to pray "Our Father" in Luke and Matthew. Those who are interested in the exegetical arguments are referred to the work of Schillebeeckx.[10]

The second actual word of Jesus is Amen. The authors of the gospels put that word into his mouth seventy-four times. Amen is translatable in different ways, but the most common translation is "let it be." If we combine those two words, their full power can be felt: Abba, Father, let it be! Speaking about God and humanity, Jesus says, "Father, let it be."

The two words contain a program of action, a working scheme, a project to be realized. Those two words involve the will of the Father, the will of the Creator, and a will Jesus came to fulfill in this world. By pronouncing those two words, or even by uttering that one word, Abba, Jesus not only reveals the core of his own personality, but at the same time, he recreates the world according to an old plan, but now in view of a new future.

This future began to outline itself more and more clearly against the horizon of our human destiny. Experts tell us how his disciples must have been very surprised when they heard him use that word Abba for the first time. Such a word, corresponding to something like our daddy, had never been used in the whole of Jewish tradition as a name for God. The first time it would be used in that way in Judaic tradition would be a thousand years later!

From time immemorial the Hebrews and the whole of traditional humanity struggled with the strange mystery hidden behind reality. They intuited the existence of something and sometimes even intuited someone. That someone, however, was in their legends and stories surrounded by a heavy curtain of purple, divine mystery. The name God was used for this intuition in some of the more recent languages. Yet it was a name without a meaning, really.

Etymologically, it seems to have been derived from a root meaning: *the one invoked*. Saying the word *God* meant no more than shouting, "Hey, you up there!" God remained a mystery. Was God good or bad, or was God both good and bad at the same time? Who would know how to approach that enigma? What to do to propitiate God?

That whole mysterious background against which Jesus' revelation about God stood out fell away for us. By his use of the word Abba, the impersonal God became personal —our affectionate parent. There is hardly anything to be bound in our modern life experience that resembles the original human fear of the tremendous, divine mystery.*

Maybe a parallel development might be found in our common daily life. Kenya, and especially its capital Nairobi, is full of refugees from other countries and abandoned children from surrounding villages.

The refugees come from Ethiopia, South Africa (called Azania by those refugees), Burundi, Ruanda, and Uganda. Those refugees are often very young. They roam through town and have nothing to do. Sometimes they are helped by the United Nations Refugee Services; sometimes they are not. Even if they are helped, that assistance means little. They get about thirty U.S. dollars a month, hardly enough to keep alive. They are constantly on the lookout for more help, on their bare feet, in trousers that are mostly torn, in a dirty shirt, and with a cardboard box under their arm which serves as their shelter for the often rather cool nights.

If you look at such a person, usually a young boy, he will come to you. If you smile at him, he will run to you and address you as Sir or Madam. He uses those terms as he does not yet know you. You are still an unfathomable mystery to him. If you listen to him, and if you help him; if you listen once more to him, and help him once more; and if you repeat the process even for a third time, unavoidably, he will make the next move. He will say, "Sir, would you mind being my father? Madam, would you like to be as a mother to me; may I call myself your son?" That Sir and Madam indicates the mystery, and with the words, father and mother, he wants to break that mystery. If you say yes, the whole situation suddenly changes. He will begin to laugh so that you can see the white of all his teeth, and he will ask for a pair of trousers. That is, naturally, his first request. After that he will ask for his other needs: food, drink, a bed, and your house. He

---

*According to speech experts, the sounds *a* and *b* are respectively the first vowel and consonant a baby can pronounce in whatever language group that baby belongs. The combination of the two sounds, abba, or baba, are used by those babies for their mother and their father. So, when Jesus told them to pray: "Our Abba, who art in heaven . . . ," no gender preference might have been meant.

became your son, didn't he? You became his parent, didn't you? If one is not careful in Africa, or in the rest of the so-called Third World, you have, in no time, a whole family of sons and daughters around you.

If anyone allows himself to be called father by a refugee, or an abandoned child, he is sold to that refugee or child. When the Sir and Madam change into Father and Mother, a totally new relationship is created.

In actual fact the whole of humanity is in flight. We are all refugees and exiles. We were all chased away from paradise. All of us are standing like refugees along the streets and roads of this world.

In all human groups in this need, people cried Sir and Madam to the mystery behind this world. In some traditions they had already shouted Father and Mother in the direction of that divine mystery before the revelation brought by Jesus Christ.

However, it was not certain whether we were allowed to do so. This became manifest only when Jesus arrived from within divinity, speaking about its mystery in a way that it had never been done before, not even in the Judaic culture. After that, we were not only permitted to address our Creator, we had to; it became our mission: *Our Father.*

Later Paul would write how the Spirit we received from Jesus made us sons and daughters of God. Jesus blew a new breath and a new spirit into us as a kind of continuation and reinforcement of the spirit that God had been blowing into us from the very beginning of our human existence.

This spirit makes us cry, "Abba, Father" (Romans 8:15; Galatians 4:6). Through Jesus Christ the divine mystery was revealed as a creative parent who cares and assists, gives life and sustains that life. Through Jesus Christ our Creator became a Father. The rest of Jesus' life is understandable only from within this Abba-revelation. He healed, he chased the devil away, he gave life to the dead, light to the blind, voice to the dumb, and hearing to the deaf. He went around as a recreating force and power, working day and night, just as his Father had done; and new life began wherever he passed. The word Abba not only recreated our human relations with

God, it also recreated our interhuman relationships. The word *Abba*, the *Our Father* pronounced by humanity, makes us into one family of mankind and God. The spirit given was presented in view of that reality.

How strange that we remain so indifferent as far as this Abba-revelation is concerned. The relationship expressed in this way seems to mean little to many of us. The difficulty does not seem to stem from accepting the parenthood of God. Who would want to miss the help, clothing, food, and drink this parenthood assures? It is the rest of the family, the whole of humanity, all those brothers and sisters, who make it difficult for us to accept the consequences of Jesus' Abba-experience in our lives. Our hesitation and indifference have something to do with our difficulty in sharing what we have with the rest of our family.

Jesus' Creative Word: Amen

God's creative words in the beginning of the Bible were all confirmed. They were spoken every time: Yes and Amen. Adam: Yes, Amen. Eve: Yes, Amen. The effect of those words was positive and good. We find that same characteristic in the recreating power of Jesus. He is on the side of a Yes and Amen to life all the time.

One morning Peter landed his boat on the shore of a lake. Jesus was waiting for him. He was waiting for some fish for breakfast. Peter had not caught anything that night. He said, "Sorry, no fish." Jesus said, "Of course there are fish, a lot of fish; just throw your net out once more, behind your boat."

Peter threw his net out again with a sigh and a wink of his eye in the direction of his comrades because of the stupid suggestion of this landlubber Jesus, the son of a carpenter, a layman. But soon fish began to swim as fast as they could from all over the lake in the direction of Peter's net. A few moments later his net and the boat were filled with fresh fish.

Jesus' mother approached him in Cana. She said, "Sorry, no wine." He said, "No wine? Of course there is plenty of wine." He directed servants to fill some jars with water and to take them to the wine steward. When the steward tasted what was in the jars, he tasted an A-grade wine so delicious that he praised the bridegroom for saving the best wine for last.

One late afternoon a whole group of hungry people were still listening to Jesus. They had listened for a long time and had been unaware of the hour. They had been too intrigued. Philip said, "The people are hungry and have nothing to eat." Jesus said, "Nothing to eat? Of course, there is plenty to eat; is there no one who has some food with him or her?" A small boy with large black eyes and an open mouth who had been looking all the time at Jesus and who had forgotten all about the food his mother had given him that morning, shouted upon hearing the questions, "Yes, Sir, here." Everyone must have laughed when he produced his three pieces of barley bread and his piece of fish from his pockets. He blushed and felt ashamed. Jesus took the food, thanked him and started to break it into pieces, a hundred, a thousand times, and the food of that boy, so small an amount that it had fit into his pockets, grew into more than a quantity sufficient for thousands.

Jairus came to him and said, "My daughter is dying; my daughter is dead. There is no life left in her." Jesus said, "Don't believe it, there is plenty of life in her; she is only asleep." Those who were there laughed at him. But when Jairus joined Jesus, they joined him too. Jesus entered the daughter's room and a few moments later she was seen sitting in the kitchen with a cup full of warm milk and a piece of mutton because Jesus had said, "Give her something to eat and drink." In their consternation they had forgotten to do that.

Again and again Jesus was the Yes and Amen. When everyone said: No, nothing. No life, no food, no drink, no hearing, no muscles, no sight, no brains, no growth, no hope, no love, he would say: Of course, there is life and food, drink and hearing, muscles and sight, brains and growth, hope and love!

Jesus told them all kinds of stories to clarify his statements, parables about a pearl hidden in a field, life sheltering in a seed, light in a bucket, a lost coin under a bed, a shekel in a fish. He pointed again and again to the positive sides of life. He was its maker and knew its possibilities better than anyone else. He knew more about its tremendous power than any of us. His most dramatic affirmation was after his death and resurrection, when he said Yes and Amen to his disciples.

His disciples were hiding, lost and nervous somewhere in Jerusalem in a room on the first floor above ground level, which is always safer than the ground floor. They thought that everything was finished. Jesus had died. They had made fools of themselves by running behind him. They thought he was a complete and sad flop, a total failure. The outcome of his life was naught and no, never. They had closed the door. They had even pushed the tables in front of them. They had closed the windows. They were like that life hidden in the seed, light under a bucket, a pearl hidden, the coin lost.

The disciples were afraid, very afraid. They hoped that all would be over in a few days' time. People would forget, they told each other. They would have to hide only for a few days, and then they would go to their normal routine work again.

That is what they thought, up to the moment when Jesus came in, giving them his recreating Spirit—to say Yes and Amen. They felt as if they were uplifted from within. Little flames of light and insight were standing on top of their heads. They suddenly discovered their undreamt-of possibilities, their content, their spirit, their vitality.

They had thought No, and he said Yes. With him all was and is possible. They began the mission he had left to them: Abba and Amen.

6

Jesus' Creative Words: Do This

While he was at the table with his disciples for their last supper before his death, Jesus took bread, thanked his Father, broke it, and said, "This is my body." He then took his chalice in the same manner, thanked his Father again, and said, "This is the chalice of my blood that is going to be shed for all," and he passed the chalice on, just as he had done with the bread. He then added, "Do this to commemorate me."

The mission Jesus gave his disciples was contained in those last words: "Do this," a task that seems to have been very often misunderstood when we look at its fulfillment around us. Isn't it true that many of us still consider ourselves faithful to Jesus' words by joining one or another in eucharist, commemorating him on a Sunday morning?

It is as if his commemoration became isolated in our lives. It became something on its own. It started to live its own life among us. Was that the intention? Was it the task he left us? Didn't the whole celebration become a kind of mere rite, a law which we should obey, a mere something, a thing?

When Jesus took the bread and wine, he was thinking about what was going to happen to him. He was thinking of his death on the cross. He was thinking of the new life he was going to introduce and create in this world. During that last supper, he was interpreting his death on the cross to his disciples. He saw his death in the light of what he once had described as his task, years before, in the small synagogue of his own home village. The people of his town had invited him to explain what he, son of a carpenter they knew so well, really wanted.

He had accepted their invitation, though it sounded a bit like a threat from the very beginning. He had waited for the reading during the Sabbath service. He was asked to do the reading. He had taken, or they had given him the scroll of Isaiah. He had accepted the scroll and had rolled it out to the text: "The Spirit of the Lord is upon me, because he has anointed me;   he has sent me to announce the good news to the poor, to proclaim release for prisoners, and recovery of sight for the blind, to let the broken victims go free, to proclaim the year of the Lord's favor" (Isaiah 61:1–2). Jesus had rolled up the scroll, had given it back to the attendant, and had sat down to indicate that he was beginning to teach. He then said "Today, in your very hearing, this text has come true" (Luke 4:18–19).

During his last supper, Jesus placed his blood, which was going to be shed, in the context he had tried to explain to John the Baptist when that prophet had sent his disciples to ask him whether he was really the Messiah. "Go and tell John what you have seen and heard: how the blind recover their sight, the lame walk, the lepers are made clean, the deaf hear, the dead are raised to life, and the Good News is preached to the poor" (Luke 7:22–23).

When he told his disciples and, consequently, us to "Do this to commemorate me," Jesus was not only referring to the breaking of bread, or the sharing of wine. His intention was not only to remain in this way in our midst. Although it is about all that, it is, however, about much more. It is about our task to participate in the bringing of the new life he came in flesh to bring from God. It is about our sharing in his creative work.

The sacrament of the Lord's supper is the healing of bodily disorder, restoration of broken relationships, elimination of social injustice, working for peace among men, and laboring to realize the new communal life that was created among us when Jesus said in the midst of us, "Our Father," making us brothers and sisters.

The Lord's supper, therefore, is an action and not a rite. It is an event that should happen here and now, and not just a memory of what happened in the past. Furthermore, it takes place outside as well as inside the church. We can go so far as to say that the vitality of us as a Christian community depends on how often it becomes a part of the event of the Lord's supper outside its own domain.[11]

Within the old human situation it must have seemed ridiculously naive even to suggest a world in which the whole of humanity would form one family. Even nowadays, almost two thousand years after Christ's death, this ideal seems to be a mere utopia.

We have only to look around in the world in which we live to come to that kind of observation. The world is divided into blocks which threaten each other with weapons that are more and more devastating every day. The world organizations are frustrated in their attempt to introduce a new economic order, UNCTAD and disarmament conferences failed, the ecumenical enthusiasm of the sixties petered out.

The total foreign debt of the Third World to the richer part of the world was estimated at $600 billion by 1983. The help given by the richer to the poorer nations is getting less and less every year. Despite the commitment of the countries organized in the Organization for Economic Cooperation and Development (OECD) to raise aid spending to the level of .7 percent of Gross National Product, the achievement of this target looks as far off as ever.

In 1981, for instance, the combined aid allocations of the OECD countries amounted to an average of .35 percent, or half of what they are committed to achieve. Over the last four years, contributions to the multilateral aid agencies have nearly halved. In 1982 the International Development Association (IDA), the soft loan arm of the World Bank that concentrates on the poorest countries and the poorest groups within them, received contributions amounting to $2.7 billion instead of the $4.1 billion it was expecting.[12]

The lack of a human family spirit is even noticeable in our personal lives. What happens to someone who refuses to join the rat race, where all compete with all? What happens to someone who is sincerely good and who corresponds to his or her creational dynamism? Even Jesus was put down because of it. He was well aware of this, as he told them during that last supper.

He was, however, also aware that his death would fail. He would rise, proving the validity and the dynamism of the new life, the life of the one divine-human community he had come to introduce. He foretold his disciples that his creative word and its creational energy would never become lost. The new spirit rooted through him too deeply in this world.

When our Creator saw Adam and Eve embracing each other, he knew all to be well, and he withdrew. At the moment that his followers marched into the world with his new spirit, Jesus knew all to be well, and in a sense he, too, withdrew to sit at the right hand of the Creator, our parent.

Implications

If the above considerations correspond to the reality as created by God and recreated by Jesus Christ, our task in this world has very serious political implications. This is true, but it is not all. It became obvious over recent years that political decisions have no impact, if another, very fundamental condition has not been fulfilled before.

It is possible to formulate a beautiful social program of equality, justice, peace, love, and unity for all. It has been done often. A nice African example is the political programming by the President of Tanzania, Julius Nyerere.

To be able to realize those programs, however, something else has to be organized in the people within those programs. First they have to convert ethically. They have to be ready to abandon their earlier attitudes and viewpoints. They have to leave those older judgements in which a human being thought only of his or her group, or only of him or herself, in order to be able to survive. It is this insight that underlies the conscientious program of Paolo Freire.

The older order no longer works. The old blocks are out. The way in which those old blocks are arming themselves against each other is the best proof of this. The only possible life pattern is the one of the new creation. Christ's new creational impulse came, as remarked earlier, when the time was ready for it. He came at a point when the development of the older creation clamored for him. He was and is necessary, absolutely necessary, then and now.

Jesus introduced a religious and a consequent ethical recreation and revolution. He did that by pronouncing his creative word *Abba* in the name of the whole of humanity. He did it by sending a new life, a new divine life for each of us. He gave us new spirituality based on a new, though often foretold, religious foundation connected to a new type of ethics asking for a new body and a new spirit.

Part III

WE
and
CREATION

7

Our Jesus Spirit

The Bible should be divided into three series of writings and documents. We divide the Bible into two parts: the Old Testament and the New Testament. It would, however, be very strange if the movement started in the Bible would have ended with two Testaments, even if we do not take the word testament in the sense of "last will," but as "witness" or "testimony." We know how the Old Testament was "executed" in the New Testament.

The New Testament has to be executed too. Its fulfillment is told in the third part, in the book of the Acts of the Apostles after the departure of Jesus, and in the writings from Paul, Peter, James, and John. Next to the Old and the New Testament we have that third testimony about the apostles, the disciples, about us. The first testimony and testament is finished. The second testimony and testament is finished, too. But the third testimony is still open. The Bible is an open-ended book.

There are at the moment some proposals, especially in Asia, to consider the Bible not as a closed book, but as a document to be complemented by holy books from other religions. That discussion is interesting, because it would also allow us to add the further adventures and experiences of followers of Jesus to the Acts of the Apostles. This is spontaneously intuited and realized every time the readings from the Bible are complemented by readings from other books during Christian meetings and liturgical services.

The history of salvation remained, for very many of us, restricted to the two first testimonies. We knew about the third phase, but we enclosed it in the second period.

In the Old Testament we read about the different periods and developments that led the Jewish people through all kinds of events to Jesus, and in the New Testament we study the life of Christ. That is the Bible for many of us.

The books contained in the New Testament that are written about the period after Jesus lose their power in this way, and they offer no further perspective as they are captured in the documents of the New Testament. There is no post-Jesus period possible. The post-Jesus period developments are seen in him. Revelation closed with the death of John.

The history of salvation, and even history in general, became fixed and stabilized. It was with that idea in their minds that missionaries and evangelists went into the rest of the world to preach a situation and a set of historical facts that very often were strange to those they met on their way, listeners who could not place those facts at all.

No wonder preaching stagnated in many places. No wonder the message often remained alienating. Growth was practically excluded. Jesus remained a good-willing stranger. The generation gap between him and contemporary man was strongly felt. Yet, we are only a distance of about two thousand years from him.

What will happen when humanity is four hundred or four thousand generations away from him? What about his Spirit in us? There are arguments to justify the encapsuling of the post-Jesus period in the Jesus phase. According to those arguments, all possible religious experiences were given in the Jesus period. New experiences or developments are practically excluded.

A well known East African scholar, John Mbiti, argued in this way. He became so impressed by Paul's saying that "Jesus died once and for all for all of us," that he suddenly got an "African" flash of insight. Professor Mbiti is of the opinion, though very many of his African colleagues disagree thoroughly, that the African does not have the idea of a future.

According to him, for an African the future is nothing but a repetition of the past. "There will be a market in town coming Wednesday, because there was a market last Wednesday, and the Wednesday before, and the Wednesday before, and so on." It was the same with Paul, Mbiti reasons, when he was thinking of salvation history. That history was past. In the present we experience the application of that past to the present.

Our salvific past will be applied to the future too. Salvation was realized in the past. The future is nothing but a further application, a further fulfillment of that past. To think of a real future, to think about something absolutely new, to visualize the possibility of new experiences is radically out. History came to an end. We are heading for a further implementation of past events.

Martin Buber considered this kind of opinion to be an essential difference between Judaism and Christianity. In Christianity the decisive event has happened already, and it can only be imitated. In Judaism "every morning is new," the future is open. For the Christian, all is settled, wrote Buber. History is finished. We can restrict ourselves to the description of experiences of the past.

In a way theologians need not even worry about what keeps them theologically busy. It is an attitude that also determines our relationship to other religious people. We have Jesus, they do not. We are saved, they are lost.

This underrating of the post-Jesus period causes another difficulty. If we don't take the post-Jesus period, the period of his Spirit among us, seriously, we restrict the relations of his disciples to him to the very individualistic and individualizing attitudes of the apostles around him during his life before his departure.

God was revealed to them in the person of Jesus. God became transparent to them through Jesus, a human being, standing next to them. They ate with him, they prayed with him, they fished with him, they walked with him. They became his friends. He became their point of reference in all they did. They admired him. They imitated him.

Those relations toward him did not make them friends of each other. That is rather obvious in the gospel stories about them. They quibbled and they squabbled. They were jealous of each other. They each wanted to sit next to him at his right side, or at least at his left side, like children and adolescents who want to sit next to a loved teacher. They discussed at length whom Jesus thought to be the most important among them. Peter was jealous of John, and John of Peter. They really did not form much of a community at the time; they were a kind of competing fan club.

Though the third part of the Bible is not without those difficulties, the followers of Jesus formed in that time a different type of community. The "external" and "outside" Jesus was away. They no longer related to each other via him as a third person. They were now themselves with his Spirit. They related to each other in that Spirit, trying to realize their community. The grouping of the non-gospel books together with the gospels may also have been one of the reasons that we kept talking too much about Jesus. Not that we should not talk about him. We should even commemorate him, as he asked us to do himself. But we continue as if he were still with us. We stared ourselves often blind on a period of time that is every day further and further away from us, and from our daily life.

In that life Jesus became a stranger, and many did not know what to do with him in their daily worries except for the hour or so they are in church Sunday morning. To them Jesus remained an outsider, an elder, a model, a parent, and their relationship to him remained childish.

The Absent Jesus

It is true that to be able to welcome the kingdom of God we must be as children. To receive human life itself is only possible as a child. It has, however, never been his intention to keep us as children. We have to grow into adulthood, also in Jesus. We have to contribute as adults to the third set of books in the Bible, books that cannot be closed as yet.

Jesus is absent in that third volume. No one ever disappeared as thoroughly from this world as Jesus, at least according to the official reports we have. There is no hair, bone, tooth, ashes, or flacon with blood left of him. It might sound irreverential, but thanks be to God that he is away. He would have hindered our development, as he himself once said: "It is better for you that I go away, because if I do not go the Spirit will not come to you" (John 16:7).

According to the reports, Jesus disappeared so radically into the sky that his departure made people living in our time of space travel suggest that he was an astronaut or someone from another planet. Yet, never did the world keep on talking so much about someone who disappeared from this earth.

It is, however, not evident that this was his intention. According to Paul, who was one of the greatest figures in the third volume of the Bible, it was not his intention. Paul observes in one of his letters to be glad never to have seen Jesus in the flesh. Those who did, according to Paul, seem to have been too busy about it. This meant also that they continued to boast about their personal, individual relations with him. They should have known by now, Paul thought, that things had changed. The Other One, the Helper, the Spirit, should have replaced him. Jesus had made a place for his Spirit in the world and in us.

That change, that transition, should take place in such a way that everyone and everything would come to its fulfillment. The bond with Jesus, of course, remained. That bond, however, was destined to grow out to a new type of relationship and attitude. We aren't very far in all that. All the time we risk seeing Jesus as a mere outsider. After his glorious and victorious departure, this difficulty should no longer be with us; the more so, as the angels who appeared to his disciples after his departure told them not to keep staring after him, but to move on, to do what he had told them to do. "Why are you standing there looking up at the sky?" (Acts 1:10). What were they going to do?

The most eloquent passages to explain their new life can be found in the most spiritualizing book of the gospels, the Gospel of John. John speaks again and again about the Helper, the Consoler, the Spirit who will come to give us fullness, maturity, insight, efficiency and community. Without that Spirit, Jesus remains a stranger to us, a visitor from another world.

The strangeness of Jesus is described in many ways. The three wise men arrived at the wrong place; they thought they would be able to find him in Jerusalem, and they had to be directed onward. Nathanael thought him so strange coming from such an insignificant location as Nazareth that he could not believe him to be anyone at all. John the Baptist speaks about the stranger in our midst. Nicodemus considers Jesus to be such a strange teacher that he dares to approach him only in the dark. The Samaritan woman addresses him as a stranger. Pontius Pilate says openly that he did not understand him.

The henchmen who nailed him to the cross were excused by him because, he said, "They don't know what they are doing." The couple walking to Emmaus walked with him all through an evening without recognizing him.

Often Jesus reacts to his being experienced as a stranger. Most times he does this by pointing to something in the people who call him strange. He reveals to them that they have something in common with him. It is as if he wants to show them a bond of like-mindedness.

Nathanael is told to be a just man. John the Baptist is asked to apply his charismatic gifts to him. Nicodemus is told that he can be reborn in the Spirit. The question of the Samaritan woman who asks him where to worship is answered by a reference to the Spirit who will take away all human alienation. Pilate is warned that he does not want to see. The henchmen are excused, as they do not see.

The couple on the way to Emmaus recognized him from within themselves, and from within the enthusiasm they felt while talking to him.

The moment they understood and had recognized him, he disappeared. They were sitting with his bread in their hands realizing that it was now up to them. Within half an hour they were on their way again to Jerusalem, not afraid of the dangers of the road they had been warning him about not so long before. Can it be possible that in our time, being on our way, we could be able to recognize him around us in such a way that we, too, can start again. If so, we will have to find that possibility in ourselves, in our own reality, just as Nathanael, Nicodemus, the Samaritan woman and the Emmaus couple did.

Interhuman Prayer

When we speak of God, we almost automatically look upward, a vertical line to God. Earth to God; we lift up our hearts to God.

That may be the reason why praying has become so difficult. An endless series of books attempts to introduce us to new and old prayer techniques. How do you obtain the necessary vertical relationship? This problem is not cleared even by our new (and therefore so very old) tricks to come to an enlarged consciousness.

Prayer should not be restricted to an exercise in verticality. Neither can it be so difficult that you are only able to do it after taking lessons. Prayer should be something natural. We do it throughout each day in our interhuman communication. It might not be surprising if we were to find out through some type of research that at least one third of our interhuman communication takes place in the form of "praying," with all the accompanying activities described so profusely in even the most classical treatises on the topic, such as adoration, thanksgiving, supplication and so on.

We communicate in many different ways. We can tell stories, and do almost all the time. We can command, but only if we have authority. We can pray. Every time we need someone over whom we have no authority, we pray to him or her. This prayer is done according to certain techniques we all know, and without them we would not survive.

The praying person par excellence is the beggar. First he tries to catch your attention. He tries to look into your eyes. If he succeeds in that, he will try to quickly build a closer communication. He will attempt that, for instance, by identifying himself: "Here are my papers; here are my documents; or here is a letter from my doctor, my minister or priest, or the welfare office. He shows his photo and that of the rest of his family. In the meantime he attentively "contemplates" his prospective benefactor. He starts by praising him: "They told me to come to you. Everyone in town knows that you never refuse to assist. You are so good, so different from the others, they told me." This praise smacks of adoration.

The next step is the supplication, which is, in fact, the core of the whole process. A prayer for forgiveness follows: "I am very sorry to waste your time; I know that you are very busy. I apologize for any inconvenience caused." A prayer of total abandonment often follows: "If you don't help, to whom should I go?" Then comes the final resolution, which is hardly ever kept, much like most resolutions: "I promise that I will spend your help very well, and I won't come back. This will be the very last time you see me!" When the "prayer" is heard, there will be a short act of thanksgiving and sometimes a devotional gift, an ex-voto in the form of a flower, handshake, picture postcard, or photo that the benefactor may keep.[13]

The behavior of a beggar is analyzed to clarify our own pattern of prayer. Isn't it true that many of us resort almost daily to this type of prayer? It is a normal interhuman activity. Some might decide to use other means, such as violence.

Our normal method is the attempt to establish community, trying to provoke in others the goodness that might open in them the willingness to enter into a kind of communion with us. It is often said that we modern people can achieve so much in the field of social, medical, economic, psychological and psychiatric care that we don't need God any more. When we are sick, we don't go to a church, we go to a specialist, and so forth.

Would it not be possible to find God in those (new?) human relationships? Did those leaders who declared themselves responsible for humanity's spiritual welfare ever seriously research that possibility? Did they ever show sufficient interest in what was going on around them? Would it really be true that God is absent from our modern human society? Did everything really grow awry among us? It is difficult to believe this. It might be that God was never found at this level of interhuman relationships simply because no one ever looked for God eye to eye.

The religious officials and professionals kept looking for God "higher up," regardless of the order given by the two angels at the occasion of Jesus' ascension. As long as God is found "high up," they are "high up," too, and can keep on looking down on others.

When the majority of contemporary humanity seems to be religiously satisfied at the interhuman level, it should be interesting to look for the reasons of their satisfaction. This type of religiosity definitely existed in Africa. In general, Africans believe in God. For many of them, however, God is far and safely away. That does not mean that they are deistic, as the famous missionary Edwin Smith thought in the beginning of this century. According to most African believers, God gave us all the power and force necessary to clear our problems and to enjoy our lives. Life itself is considered to be God's most important gift.

We should not refer too often to God, they say. It is not good to have recourse to God except in the case of dire need. There are many proverbs to express that belief. It is not wise to show one's face too often to a chief.

Many theologians and church leaders will immediately remark that in this way the interhuman, horizontal line will prevail over the vertical line, the line by which we are connected to God. They are right. But, so what? There is an African answer to the question: "Isn't there the danger that we are getting too horizontal, that we forget about God, that we neglect the vertical connection?" Their answer: Is God so weak that he needs to be defended by us? Can't God fend for himself?

Some African scholars have been reacting more radically to this issue. Reflecting on the religion and theology imported from the West, they have become both upset and angry. They maintain that the almost exclusive "vertical" religious attitudes preached by the evangelists and missionaries explain why the church did practically nothing against the colonial rule.

The imported vertical relationship drew all the attention to a kingdom not situated here on earth but somewhere up there in heaven. This verticality, not completely unknown to the Africans but hardly stressed in their worship, devitalized the people. It sapped their strength and made them inactive in this world. It became a tool to oppress.

If we are not allowed to look for God within *ourselves*, then he must remain above us or next to us.

The discussion could be endless and in a sense fruitless, too, as it does not touch the real issue as to whether there is a divine dimension at our interhuman level of communication.

Jesus said, "The kindom of heaven is in your midst." When he said this he was speaking not only to his disciples but to the people around him. Pharisees included.

If Jesus promised to send his Spirit to be with us, wouldn't we be able to recognize it among us?

When we "pray to each other," we are inviting each other to communion and community. Real community, according to Jesus and John, is the work of the Holy Spirit. While praying to each other we call forth solidarity, comradeship, and love in each other. In our holy books all good comes from God, from God's activity in us since the moment of our creation.

"Praying to each other" is praying in the most authentic sense of the word. It is contacting God. It is asking for God. It is the building of God's temple. It is the bringing together of each other in God. It is something that rests on a reality present in each human being, though often it remains hidden.

Why don't our theologians live with their eyes wide open and look at what is happening around them? Every time people pray to each other, the Spirit is awakened, community is asked for. Our life is full of Spirit, the "in-between" God.

Spirit Experience

Divine disclosures can no longer take place in Jesus. He is away. They don't seem to happen too often in our direct, vertical communication with God any more either.

It is difficult to get exact data on this type of experience. Few are interested in this type of research, although now and then some study is done. In 1973 the Catholic bishops of the United States published the results of such a study: "Spiritual Renewal of the American Priesthood."[14] Page forty-five of the booklet offers some interesting details. Fifty-six percent of the priests who had been asked whether they had ever experienced God in their lives answered Yes, frequently. Twenty-five percent confessed to "mystical experience," viz "the overwhelming feeling of being one with God."

The report showed that there was no correlation between those experiences and the prayer life of the priests. Whether they did their regular spiritual prayer exercises or not made no difference. Only one correlation was revealed. The priests who did not relate well to the human community around them barely experienced the presence of God in their lives.

What is true of priests is true of all. It is in our relation to others that we experience God in our lives. If those relations do not exist or are very feeble, the experience of God becomes difficult.

Contemporary spiritual authors have been stressing, repeating what older writers have often said before, that priests should try to find the source of their spiritual life in their pastoral activities. When we translate such a piece of advice in view of non-clerics, it means that they, too, should find their spiritual experience in their daily lives and activities.

What are the religious dimensions found in one's life? One of them, as explained above, is the spiritual experience we can find in our "interhuman prayer," a prayer that never stops, and in our interhuman solidarity, sociality, and love.

Sometimes we do things that are absolutely beyond us. One explanation is that we don't know the full extent of our human possibilities and, therefore, don't use them. Medical researchers agree that we use only a fraction of our brain power, though they don't agree on the percentage we engage already. Yet, shouldn't we admit now and then that miracles seem to happen to and through us?

Sometimes we think that the time of miracles is past. That time will only be past at the moment when we have a full insight into all our human potentialities, including those powers given to us with the Spirit. That knowledge and insight are not yet acquired. We still live partly in the dark. Even nowadays miraculous healings take place through the intervention of those who pray, laying on their hands, as well as by medical doctors.

At times, bits of advice are given that surpass the wisdom of the advisers. All of us have spoken words we thought we would never be able to speak. We have witnessed how people around us are able to forgive each other in situations where such a forgiveness seemed impossible. Endless quarrels suddenly ended. Sinful human organizational patterns such as slavery disappeared overnight from this earth. (Let us pray and believe that our armament race will one day go the same way; and it will!)

Much depends on how one interprets such events and experiences. It is possible to see them in the light of Paul's *exousia*, "Something, a power went out from me." That something, that power, built community in a very special way.

The Spirit we received not only lives at our individual level. The Spirit is not only for me. The Spirit is one of love, a community builder. The Spirit wants to connect us. That activity is functional. We are with the Spirit in view of others.

To express this in the traditional Pauline manner: We have our charisms, each of us has her or his charisms. All people should be able to do what priests are supposed to do —the doctor who healed a sick person, the mother who helped her son over a critical point, the car mechanic who did a splendid job, the street cleaner who swept the pavement efficiently, the scholar who suddenly found a solution to a problem. All of them should find the source of their spiritual experiences in daily activities and functions.

Why has this not been sufficiently explained? Why do people think that spirituality is something reserved for a certain class of people? Why does that class single itself out as if they were the lone possessors of those powers?

The whole development of humanity should be seen in this light. It should be a support for youth preparing for life, trying to find out about their role and charism; it should be a comfort in our old age.

When Jesus Christ had lived under the influence and with that spirit for about thirty-three years, he was left with wounds in his hands, his feet, and his heart. This will happen to each of us who lived in that spirit. As in the case of Jesus, it is difficult and frustrating to work at building the kingdom of God among us. There are too many opposing and negative forces. Neither our imagination nor our belief was developed sufficiently. We lived too easily; we looked only for simple and quick solutions at a short distance. We did not tackle our problems well enough. For that reason we are surrounded by refugees, victims, oppressed people and oppressors, and all kinds of inhumanities. Everyone meets injustices, violence, discrimination, egoism and prejudices in life.

It may sound pious, but our human existence is a "crucifying" experience, at least for those who live with their eyes open.

Some of the spiritual phenomena in our world are very strange. Anyone interested in these matters knows that all over the world Pentecostal and charismatic movements started in and outside the churches, accompanied by miracles, healings, conversions, but also by less "normal" activities such as speaking in tongues. According to theologians who studied this phenomenon, the gift of tongues has been lacking in the churches since apostolic times. Now it has started again.

All over the world, participants in prayer meetings stand up and speak in tongues. Psychologists who have researched the matter, say that it happens especially to people who have no chance to speak during their daily lives. A clerk who has to keep his mouth shut all through the week in his office and a factory worker whose opinion is never solicited at home, at work, or anywhere else would suddenly burst into that kind of free flow speech if stimulated in a somewhat religious or social context.

The psychologists present an interpretation in which the Spirit is absent. Others maintain that the gift of tongues is the most significant sign of the presence of the Spirit in our days. Maybe both opinions can be combined.

The one who finds expression during the speaking of tongues did remain unnoticed for too long. The Spirit, up to now neglected and misunderstood, draws attention to itself. A kind of protest might be coming from the Spirit, which refuses to remain inactive and unnoticed any longer. There is another way to illustrate and clarify our point.

Jesus gave a description of what he left to us, a reality which he called, somewhat under the influence of his own time and culture, his kingdom. What is that kingdom exactly? It is a type of human community described by Jesus, for instance in the Gospel of Matthew, chapters five, six, and seven.

The description is what we would call a counter culture. In those chapters we find a collection of sayings and speeches by Jesus depicting a world that is very different from the world we have organized around ourselves today. In that collection of talks Jesus asks us to direct our prayers to Our Father; and as explained in a preceding chapter, this prayer put us straight away into the midst of our human community. An exhortation to pay attention to the building out of solidarity, and interhuman justice and love follow. The collection starts with the eight beatitudes.

Those beatitudes should be seen within the framework of the rest of the talks; otherwise, they seem to be pious and nice but rather impractical. Within the context of the rest of the commands given by Jesus, they become very realistic and also, in a sense, hard hitting. That we have to be the "salt" and the "light" of the earth sounds pleasant, but things become serious when Jesus speaks about our clothing, our time, our money, and our relations to others. We have to be related to those others in such a way that in our solidarity our left hand should not even know what our right hand is doing.

After the treatment of those issues, the meaning of the

eight beatitudes becomes clearer. They should be seen in a spiritual context as indicated by the beginning of each beatitude, "Blessed are they . . . ." At the same time they indicate where we have to look for our spiritual experiences.

In all eight beatitudes we are invited to provoke in and around ourselves the Spirit that brings us together in solidarity: blessed are they who know their need for God, who are sorrowful, who are gentle, who hunger and thirst to see right prevail, who show mercy, whose hearts are pure, the peacemakers, they who have suffered persecution for the cause of right.

In a kind of preview of the final judgment from the hand of the same Matthew, this solidarity is the only norm by which we will be judged. The norm in that last ordeal is not whether we "knew" or "recognized" Jesus. It is something else. It is about the acceptance or refusal of community.

Many who ended up on the right side say very honestly, "You say that I helped you when you were hungry, when you were thirsty, when you were in prison, when you were sick; but I never saw you." He answers them, "I tell you this, anything you did for one of my brothers here, however humble, you did for me."

They were taken up in the kingdom because they had organized their lives and affairs in such a way that they already belonged to it here on earth in the Spirit, who brought them together.

8

Our Jesus Body

He took the bread, broke it, and said: "This is my body." He took the chalice with wine, handed it around, and said: "This is my blood."

What body was Jesus speaking of when he said this? This might seem an odd question, but it isn't. Our ideas about our body and about our bodiliness have been changing considerably over the centuries.

A Pygmy in a Zairean rain forest experiences the whole of the forest, sky, sun, and moon as belonging to his body. Such a Pygmy does not see himself as bodily apart from his surroundings.

The classical individualized Western person thinks of his or her body as all that goes on between the top of the head and the soles of the feet, or between the finger tips of the right hand to the finger tips of the left.

For many of us, our bodiliness is more extended than that. We have all kinds of eye-, ear-, mouth-, and even heart-enhancers. We use eyeglasses, telescopes, television, telephones, hearing aids, megaphones and false teeth. We may have silver and steel pins installed in our bodies to keep us together, plastic joints and parts of bones, nerve- and sense-amplifiers, steel skull strengtheners, and even artificial hearts.

Bicycles, motorbikes, cars, planes, gliders and surfboards are often felt as enlargements, or more or less integrated parts of our own bodies. This feeling is common to the teenager who races his motorbike along the road with his throttle wide open, or to the car driver who feels the size of her vehicle as if it were an extension of her body as she tries to find her way through busy traffic. These examples are mechanical body-extensions.

Some other aspects should be mentioned. Much of our evolved sense of bodiliness has something to do with our contact with fellow human beings. Especially our communication is increasing. We no longer live in the singular; we live in the plural.

Notwithstanding the often too lyrical and utopian description, it is indeed true that we human beings have been getting so near to each other through all the channels that bring us together that we have started to speak of *our* human interests and, in fact, of our one unifying body.

We are using our resources more and more commonly. We eat food from all over the world; our energy might come from totally different sources than our own. If any group of human beings were not connected to this general network, it hardly can be considered to be participating in human life.

Our organizational networks are growing every day. Speaking about organization, one is to speak about a reality where body and mind intermix. To explain what an "organization" really is, is difficult. It is definitely not something purely of the mind.

We came into a kind of development in which the human identity, up to very recently, identified as a very clearly circumscribed "I," starts to reveal itself more and more as a "We." This same evolutionary concept might be expressed in words that sound maybe less fortunate: We human individuals are becoming humanity.

The most varied observers of human nature have recently come to this kind of discovery. The existentialist, Sartre, who spoke about an organic universal humanity; the paleontologist, Teilhard de Chardin, who observed that human individuals are becoming parts in one human organism; and the psychoanalyst, Jung, who believed that the only valid modern model for God is the Spirit descending upon all and uniting us together; all share variations of the same opinion.

Old Fear

The reaction to these developments is very often fear. There is a fear that the individual human being will fall away, will be dissolved. The fear that, instead of making a step toward a new kind of human society in which each person will find personal fulfillment in relation to all the others, we are making a step backward to a primitive collectivity in which no one was anyone as an individual nor would be able to become one either.

Are we human beings, modern urban dwellers, on the way to a global village? As most people came to town to escape from their village situation with its social pressures and control, the idea does not seem to be very attractive. At first sight the new bodiliness does not seem to be so very new. Didn't old humanity, divided over small ethnic groupings, form such a kind of bodiy togetherness?

In the oldest human communities of this world, the clan members were connected in a way that seemed to exclude all individuality. The clan and its taboos seemed to overrule, not only personal initiative, but even any trace of individuality.

When a child in such a group is asked for its name, it will give first its clan name, and only afterward, if one insists, its personal name. In our regions, a child asked for its name will give first its own name, and only afterward its family name.

Those older systems knew of a kind of participatory bodiliness. There were obvious advantages. One shared one's food, bananas, sorgum, or whatever one had to eat and drink. No one in the clan was hungry as long as anyone in the clan had something to eat. The restrictions of this organizational pattern were, however, such that they led to urbanization in the so-called Third World. Town is a liberation to very many. It always has been.

Most of us did not leave our old, more rural pattern so very long ago. We would not like to go back there though we might feel now and then a nostalgia for certain aspects of it, such as its communality and its security. So often we hear about the threats of a totally collectivized future and about the threat of Orwell's 1984, that McLuhan's prophecy about the future global village means bad news to most of us.

Believing Christians, however, might try to see these developments in the light Jesus brought into this world. An English monk, Sebastian Moore, and the neo-Marxist utopian, Ernst Bloch, drew attention to the self-definitions Jesus gave, definitions we all know and which have been repeated all through the last twenty centuries.

When Jesus spoke about his "I," he described that "I" as a part of a whole. It was part of the vine, for instance. He was the trunk; we are the branches. He is described as the head of a body. He was the most important part, the head; but he was ony a part, and what can the head do without the rest of the body?

We knew that after his death and resurrection the *risen* Jesus Christ is present in the bread and the wine of our eucharistic services. We did not always draw the conclusions of our belief. Teilhard de Chardin did.

One day while sitting in front of a tabernacle in a Roman Catholic Church, he suddenly realized in a kind of vision that the consecrated bread in that tabernacle not only became Jesus of Nazareth. He saw that in him the whole of creation was present, the whole of humanity.

We knew about this "wholeness" in faith. Maybe we didn't draw the consequences because we didn't know about our human situation. That situation is better understood every day. We know now, from an empirical point of view, that we belong together sociologically, economically, psychologically, and even medically. However, it remains difficult to put this "belonging" into the practice of our daily lives.

Up to now it was only seen in the light of faith. We have to find the courage to be ourselves and to be at the same time part of the whole. It is this courage which will bring us together as one humanity.

Self Development

Many will say, "We've heard this before." They are right. The idea is not new. In the expectation of humanity, it is most probably as old as humanity itself. In the reality of human life, it is at least 2000 years old. Yet, it remains so new that it still sounds like an illusion. It will remain an illusion until we stop only talking about it in our ecclesial and theological gatherings. Reflection will remain necessary.

Prayer is as much needed as bread. It is necessary in view of that bread. It is in our prayer that we might come to the realization of what our liturgy means and asks from us. Prayer is necessary to ensure each one in this world his or her piece of bread. Talks and meditations do not fill stomachs. Besides those talks and meditations are often too individualistically directed. That was due to the pattern in which we have been caught. Each of us has our individual relation to Jesus. We work wonders of goodness toward others. Missionaries are willing to go out to save one soul.

We pay little attention to the individual as part of a whole. We stress that Jesus came to save each of us, personally, and are quite willing to accept him as our personal savior. We hardly ever realize that Jesus had come for the whole of humanity, that he was dedicated to human life as such. His dedication should become our dedication. His dedication is hardly developed in our church context.

Within our churches we continue to think about ourselves and of our personal salvation. We try to come to our personal and group fulfillment. We have not succeeded. We will never succeed in this way. We simply don't live up to our very nature. We keep on missing the mark, which evangelically means that we remain sinners. We remain alienated from ourselves.

It will be difficult to change this. The structures we live with hinder us in our development. This is true for the smaller structural units such as family, business, etc., as well as our larger units, such as nation, church, defense, organization, etc.

The breaking and sharing of the bread and wine as proposed and intitiated by Jesus cannot be but subversive in as far as our actual structures are concerned. His breaking and sharing pointed toward totally different relationships. They not only pointed toward them, they also realized them.

Those new relationships are the mission he left us. That is the temple he asks us to build. That is the body that counts. That is the development aid we have to render each other.

Speaking of development, we often think of others, such as the Third World as needing to be developed (as if we, ourselves, don't need further developing). If Jesus Christ left us the task to form one people of God, one temple, one body, we, too, still have much to develop.

We have to grow in the execution of that mission. No one can be a "full" Christian before this task has been completed. All of us are blind, deaf, dumb, and crippled until that assignment has been fulfilled. All of us are underdeveloped.

Obstructions

Many of us, at this moment, live in a kind of Indian summer of our individuality. We think we will be able to save our bodies and our souls in this way. Most probably, we will in the hereafter. God's mercy is immense. We won't however, here and now. No one can save himself or herself in isolation any more.

The idea of piercing anyone's eardrums goes against the human rights of that person. Everyone has the right to hear and to communicate with others. The same right would be violated if the hearing aid were to be taken away from a practically deaf person. Wouldn't one infringe on the same rights if one person denies another the use of telephone, radio, and television?

All those vehicles of communication are, within our context, necessary to survive and to participate. Our life has become more "communal" than we often suspect.

To a great extent, we are already forming one wholeness. It is from this point of view that we have to reconsider our ideas about development. Our aid to others is no longer either charity or justice. When my hand is taking care of my eye, I don't speak about charity or justice either. Those categories don't come into play in such cases. It is a normal instinctive survival reflex.

It should be the same within the general human bodily framework. If we take our common bodiliness seriously, we should be able to accept the consequences. It would be evangelically appropriate to do so. One body and one spirit are unquestionably gospel themes.

This does not mean that our personalities would fall away. It would mean that our pure individuality would disappear. We should think of ourselves as part of a world community, no longer individual, if the latter had, indeed, been possible before. Our difficulty as modern Christians is that we want to socialize and remain as individuals at the same time.

It is understandable that there will be a desperate revival of individualism on the threshold of our socialization. What one defends most quickly is often most quickly lost. A certain degree of obstinacy is often an indication that one already knows the heritage to be lost. It is this insight that might help us to explain much of what happened to us in the past.

We should see the present happenings in the same light. The person who is going to die of cancer will have a short redress just before his death. The shop that was going to close revives just before the bankruptcy. It was even decided to give the shop a new face lift because of it.

The difficulties we experience regarding the new communalism are not only in the personal field. They exist also for groups that are self centered in their aims and goals. This kind of "fascist" exclusivism will be experienced more and more as sinful. It is strange and significant that the idea of purely individualistic sins is disappearing rather rapidly.

We start to understand better and better that hardly any of our sins are committed with "our full knowledge and free will." We know the extent to which we are who we are because of the structures in which we try to survive. It is rather tragic that this new dimension of sin is not yet fully understood. Sin is, and remains, an individual and social act.

We stick too much to an impossible social ideal, impossible because the individual privileges that were once feasible are no longer possible or acceptable. In as far as our old setup obstructs further development, our structures are sinful. They make us miss the mark. They are sins against the Holy Spirit who wants to bring us together.

Dedication to His Body

The vision of Jesus of Nazareth is obvious. In his vision all human beings are a part of one whole. That wholeness is the human being for which he opted. It is the wholeness in which each human being will find her-, or himself. It is the end of alienation. To cooperate in that humanization and incarnation is our task; it is also the liturgy we are asked to organize.

In the beginning of this chapter we asked ourselves: what body was Jesus speaking about, when he broke his bread saying, "This is my body!" Two prayers during our communion services offer an answer.

We not only ask God to change the bread and the wine into the body and blood of our Lord Jesus; we also invoke the Holy Spirit to change the faithful into the one body of Christ. Both prayers are heard, when the tension between the two is lifted, when we share in the bread and the wine. Jesus Christ is fully present physically and spiritually in the community of the living and the dead. As those present break the bread and share in this way, they unite with him and in him, the new *body of humanity*.

This new human bodiliness, however, to a great extent, still remains our task. What is realized during such a celebration of communion is not very much more than a model and a project when compared with the reality of our daily lives. It is a bodiliness "under construction."

Every commemoration of the last supper is an expression of that faith, a faith not yet fully expressed as we celebrate our eucharistic services. The way in which we have been celebrating them can only have been provisional. All our celebrations up to now have been group celebrations. Within those groups we have been celebrating group values. We ate together with some, we celebrated with some; others were excluded. They were not allowed to participate, to communicate.

Our celebrations should be more universal and much

less exclusive or not exclusive at all if we really want to do what Jesus intended to do among us. Each human being belongs to the body of the whole. The solidarity asked from us is the organic unity of all humanity. It means the end to the aims of any one group! It implies a cross through all forms of egoistic individuality.

The consequences of this mission are obvious. In the practice of our daily lives, this mission is thwarted by the problems that have haunted humankind from the beginning of modern times: war, peace, welfare, abundance, scarcity, wealth, poverty, hunger and thirst, exploitation, and all of our psychological, economical, social, rural, and transport problems.

We are facing what John in his Book of Revelation calls the issue of building the one new town; the problems of building that *polis* and the politics involved. It is as if the spiritual life of many contemporary religious people, Christians included, became stuck.

That is one of the reasons this book on spirituality was designed. It is as if a genuine perspective and vision are missing. That is not completely true or the idea of planning this book would not have been possible.

It is, however, true that we seem to be in a change-over. We are switching, and it happens often that when we switch, power and light fall out for a short period. One is for a brief time in the dark. For a few moments the machinery comes to a standstill. A motor does not really pull at the moment we are changing our gears. We will get through the interruption; we will emerge from the dark.

It does no good only to moan about what we see around us. It is useless to put all our energy in laments and sighs. The new vision, the new insight, the new certainty in the form of the new hope are with us, although we still have to get accustomed to them in the practice of our lives.

After the change-over, many of the things we were accustomed to in the period before will be able to continue. They will have to be renewed, they will have to be seen in the new light, but they will survive.

Let us consider some of the classical attitudes Christians have always been nourishing in their lives. In their dedication to the body of Jesus, many Christians have been practising evangelical poverty. They did this to imitate Jesus, to bring out in themselves the spirit of Jesus, but they did it also to be able to help others. This dedication to poverty, should now be done in a different way, at another frequency, with another color. We should no longer speak of poverty, not even in this context. Poverty is undesired, unwanted; it is a disaster for those who are really poor. It means misery. We should be trying to combat that misery all over the world.

What the more religious people among us used to call evangelical poverty, to which everyone, Christian or non-Christian is called, might now be described as that life attitude in which each of us lives consciously in a simple way in view of the one body we form. That body is the reason we break our bread, that we share what we have with others. Those who dedicate themselves to this one body, seen by them as the body of Jesus Christ, have to show their dedication in this way.

The same idea applies to that other evangelical attitude "obedience." It would be very difficult to live only by one's own individual insight and light and yet to cooperate in the wanted solidarity and unity within the body. Nor is it any longer permitted to submit oneself only to the insight and light of one person in authority.

Within the one Spirit that binds us together in the one body, we will have to listen to that Spirit in each other. This listening, this living by a shared and participated insight, is the new form of obedience to the will of God. It is not exactly what we call democracy. It is not what normally happens when we speak of democracy. It is not a simple counting of noses. It is a clear and deliberate attempt to discern the Spirit in us.

It is, to use a rather awkward word: *Pneuma-cracy.* It is the end to those situations where we speak about superiors and, consequently, about inferiors. It is the end to all masterships, an end already announced by Jesus two thousand years ago.

And if there are those who would like to remain unmarried in view of this body, then their choice will make
sense only in as far as they remain unmarried to wed
themselves to this new body. That body should also give
meaning to the marriage of those who wed and continue
human life in that image.

The Revised Assignment

The point at issue is one people, one temple, one
body. The living, the dead, and those still to be born will all
be alive in this wholeness. All and everything should be
oriented toward it. This goal should be worked out with all
the faithful. They should be better informed about it. If all
live and work in that direction, our world will change.

Our modern spiritual world is buzzing with activity,
revision, and reform. This continued activity and excitement
seem to indicate that we have not yet found our way. The
changes and reforms introduced do not seem to solve our
problems. Wouldn't the reason be that so many of those revi-
sions are oriented toward the individual, even when they take
place in the context of group sessions?

Shouldn't we pluck up the courage to make his body
and Spirit our real issue? The latter kind of reorientation is
not only desirable within our personal sphere, it is necessary
within our churches as well. It is necessary all over. All
groups in the world should open to all. No group should remain closed. We should welcome all others in our endeavors
to grow into him.

Should the name of Jesus be used in this work? The
believing Christian witnesses that the Spirit has been given to
all from the very beginning, from the moment of creation.
We should be able to recognize each other as brothers and
sisters in the Spirit, which at a certain point should be named.
In its divine and human fullness its name is Jesus. We can and
should say this as long as his name does not estrange others
from us.

We don't differ in the Spirit. We don't even differ in
the way we contradict that Spirit. The difference between us

is not spiritual; the difference is physical, a bodily handicap. Jesus is already the head of the new humanity, body and blood; but we are still nonfunctioning members, like disconnected organs. What is lacking is our bodily integration. Our personal egoism and our group "fascism" are blocking us. The Gypsies in Europe say that our sin is the repression of our brothers and sisters. They know what they are talking about.

This revised assignment does not mean only that we should be politically engaged in justice, love, peace, and unity. It implies these politics without doubt. Also, it means a change in each of us, a *metanoia* that should influence our daily behavior at home, in the garden and the kitchen, in our schools, churches, and hospitals, in our businesses, and in all our decisions.

Peacemakers have always been venerated. Jesus had a very special praise for them. Our peacemakers should be the builders of bridges over which the Spirit of God will bring us together, notwithstanding the difficulties of the past, to form one temple, one body of God now and in all time to come.

9

Program and Action

In the Book of Wisdom (sometimes called The Wisdom of Solomon), God is called a lover of life, and the text adds: Your imperishable breath is in all life (Wisdom 11:26, 12:1). The life meant is human life. Human life, as such, is something abstract. It does not exist. Creation is about the life of concrete men and women.

It is this life that God calls good. "All existing things are dear to you, and you hate nothing you have created—why else would you have made it? How could anything have continued in existence, had it not been your will? How could it have endured unless called into being by you?" (Wisdom 11:23–26).

In the creation story, human life is the center. Anything that would take human life out of the center of our attention is dangerous to that life. Life can be frustrated, or boycotted in two ways.

The first, as was mentioned earlier, is that we consider "things," the products of our own hands and minds, as the center of our interest.

The second is that we restrict our interest in human life to that of a particular group, creating a kind of apartheid and inequality that contradicts the original creational act rather than thinking as we should in terms of human life as a totality.

Both ways are mistakes which are continually being made. In the North (West), things are used as theoretical models to explain reality. In the South (Africa), personified forces were used with the same intention. In both cases one hoped to be able to explain the world. In both cases one succeeded to a considerable extent. Explanations were needed in view of the organization and the quantitative and qualitative growth of human life. It all started in good faith, in view of human life.

Notwithstanding threats and warnings, humanity in the North put things in the center of their worship, while humanity in the South put spirits into the center of theirs. Creational reality was lost and out of sight. Superstition entered. Life's meaning was neglected.

The second mistake—when almost every human group started to cut life down to the size of only its own group—gave birth to economic differences. Every group considered itself unique, at least as very special and apart. Even within those groups, the interest in the general welfare of the group often fell away so that egoism and individualism prevailed.

Classes began to exist; the differences between the rich and the poor, the rich countries and the poor countries, arose. These differences would lead to a division of the world into a first, second, and third worlds. comprising hundreds of sovereign nations.

The situation has become so complicated because we are caught in various ways. The rich are frustrated and anxious because they are oppressed by the things in their lives. They are slaves of the fleshpots of Egypt.

The poor, who most probably are free from the oppression of things only because they are poor, are oppressed by the rich.

As noted already, each human being seems to be a refugee. Also, everyone is oppressed, a slave. We are not only enslaved by the structures we allow to grow among us, like the multinationals and the nations with their security organizations, we are also crushed within ourselves. We are not free, either in ourselves, or in our lives.

We are abused by overwork, by control of business, by rule of our appointment books, which are so much more important than our lives, that we are ready to sacrifice our lives to them. We are not ourselves; we don't know our own life extent because we are restricted to the group to which we belong, looking with the utmost of suspicion at others around us. Humanity is caught in a very old land, the old Egypt of the Bible.

A Simple Solution

Theoretically, a solution is simple to find. If the above issue were the subject of an essay competition, the answers would flow in very easily.

To liberate their humanity, those who are caught should drop the things and put their own lives as the center of interest. They should choose for a simple and healthy life. Small is even more beautiful than ever visualized before. They should work less, divide their work among many more hands and heads, and reduce their business.

In that way it would be possible to diminish the group differences, economic and social inequalities included; tensions would disappear, and life's optimum would increase for all, even for those who live marginally now.

Less or no money would have to be spent on armament, aggression, and self defense. It would mean that humanity would gather, so to speak, around one table and eating together would form more as one human family. It would also mean that our survival chances in this world would increase.

Actually, it is the only way in which we can assure our future and, at the same time, rescue our past. If humanity fails in this world, our past fails too. All the efforts and developments of our ancestors, our foremothers, and forefathers would have been in vain.

Such a failure would imply that God's creation would fail, that God's creational words would return in vain. But God's words do not turn back empty. Jesus proved this by the simplicity of his life. He believed passionately in human life and its inborn goodness. He was liberated from any belief in "things"; he was free from all possible types of superstition.

He declared the human family to be one, and he invited everyone to eat and live together. At least twice he organized enormous picnics in the open field as signs of this future.

He demonstrated by his way of life and by many miraculous works that his life came directly from our Creator, and that what he did was in the line of everything his Father had ever done before for human life. He revived the original goodness in us. He referred to a promised land.

The Need for New Leadership

Many of us have given up. We have surrendered to the actual situation. Some of us hope for something hereafter; many don't believe that either. Some are waiting and say continually, "We will see." Some are preparing for the big blast or, as others say, for the crunch. It is useless to dream of a new beginning. The world and humanity are too old. We are living on a dying star. Our politics have become a joke, a sick one. Religion is waning and on the way out. An unavoidable fate has hit us all.

We reason like the Hebrews in Egypt. When Moses said: We can do something about it, we can change the situation, we are created by God, we are not forsaken by God, we are meant to live! They told him to shut up. Any change or revolution, any resistance would aggravate the situation. They continued their slavework, they continued to register their newly born sons for death. They chased Moses away. They wanted nothing to do with him and his projects. He was crazy.

Finally, Moses did manage to win them over for their new future. He rescued them from the fate that hung over their heads and in their hearts. In modern English jargon, leaders are sometimes called de-fatalizers. The leader is the one who neutralizes any doom thinking. That is what Moses did for them.

The same language was heard around Jesus. It was his family who started. Even his mother took part in it. They came to tell him that he had to be more prudent. "Play it cool," they said; "Don't exaggerate." Peter told him a thing like that should never happen to him. Caiphas accused him. Herod laughed. Pilate was doubtful. Pilate's wife wept in fear. Jesus' disciples ran away. Judas gave up on him. His mother stood under the cross. Nicodemus buried him. The soldiers sealed the tomb. The couple walking to Emmaus were honest enough to admit they had such great hopes in him. Mary asked the gardener, "Where did you put him?"

And for about three days, all remained silent. The new life Jesus had introduced had been killed by the old life. A decision had been made long before his arrest, condemnation, and death on the cross—a decision made in meeting rooms, palaces, and living rooms all over the country. They all had said, "This is impossible. It can't end well. His type of life is nice for the birds he seemed to like so much. No human being can live like that. Let us keep to the old, it isn't too bad, you know."

After three days, he reappeared! He had been right. They had been wrong. The new life was not only possible, he was expressing the new creation. He was the new, creative word. The old life had been de-fatalized. Everything was going to be new, everything was going to be possible. The proof had been given.

He even repeated what his Father had done to Adam and Eve. God had breathed life into their being. The same day Jesus rose, he visited his disciples who were scared stiff when they saw him. Maybe they were not frightened so much because they saw him, but because they realized that the life he had come to introduce was going to be theirs from then onwards. He saw their fear. He said, "Peace." He repeated, "Peace!" And then, reminding them of that old story in the beginning of their holy book, he breathed over them, blowing his new life deep into their very beings.

At this point of our human history, a type of doom consciousness seems to have mesmerized us again. This time it hit not only one human group. It hit the whole of humanity. Aren't many of us simply waiting for the end? Aren't many of us thinking that we know how the end will come?

It is present in the personal lives of so many—in the acceptance, without resistance, of the rat race; in being content, without reservation, with a flat, one-dimensional way of life. We are sacrificing ourselves, we are sacrificing our children, we are sacrificing life. We are sitting around the fleshpots. We are looking, but we don't see. We are hearing, but we don't listen. And the rich are getting richer while the poor are getting poorer.

We do need new leaders, or better, we need new prophets. It has to be possible to escape from this perplexity. It must be possible to undo doom thinking. The followers of Jesus should believe that it is possible because of him and in him. Many Christians, however, don't seem to believe that any more. It is often not their fault. The blame often lies with the leadership. The old canons and catechisms seem to have had their time.

The Story of Those Invited for the Celebration

In a well-known parable Jesus explains how people relate to the life to which the Father invites us. It is the story of the guests invited for a wedding banquet organized by the king for his son. The guests reacted in different ways. Some of them did not come at all. They were not interested. They did not understand the invitation. One went to his farm to count his cows. Another had to try out a new oxen-cart. A third one was busy stock-taking in his business. Some even went so far that they troubled his messengers. They did not see. They were blind and foolish, focused only on "things."

The host, rather upset about their behavior, decided to invite others so as not to disappoint his son. He sent his messengers out again, and they collected all they could find, good and bad alike (Matthew 22:10). The hall was packed with guests. When the king came in, he sat down at a table and looked around. He was very happy to see that so many had come to celebrate with him. He observed his guests, the good ones and the bad ones—the good ones who always had been kind to life, and the bad ones who had now and then treated it very badly.

Then, according to Jesus' story, he did something extraordinary. Did he throw out the good ones? Of course not. Did he throw out the bad ones? No, he did not do that either. There was only one person he had removed from the hall, the one who had come in without having been dressed properly for the celebration. The man had accepted the invitation. He had joined the messengers but had not believed them. That was the reason he had not gone home to change. He was thrown out because he had not believed, because he had no hope, because he had no vision. He was thrown out to be with those who had not even come because they had not been interested. Don't we often seem to be hopeless like him?

Utopia or Advent

From all over, experts are regularly coming to the world's centers to dream their dreams. They come for conferences and symposia, for workshops, and brainstorming sessions. They attend meetings of the World Bank, of the International Monetary Fund, Unctad, Unesco, Unep, Fao, and so on.

Christians come together in the World Council of Churches in their denominational and international meetings in Geneva, Rome, Pasadena, New Delhi, and Nairobi. The participants of those meetings hope to change the world. In one way or another they are all inspired by the idea and the ideal that one day the whole of humanity will be one.

They come together full of hope for that new life, expecting a splendid future. In all those cases the world and humanity resemble—to use an authentic and old biblical image—a young girl, a splendid woman, a virgin full of promise, full of dreams. The new Jerusalem. Wasn't Jerusalem the name of a girl? Doesn't that name mean something like "the bearer of peace"?

According to the Bible, the world without God is sterile, unfruitful, and in chaos. We are told this in many ways. Take all of the great women, our foremothers, in those old stories. Sarah, the woman of Abraham, was barren. Abraham, who lived with a promise that his offspring would be as numerous as the stars in heaven, had a woman who was a dry as a piece of wood lying in the desert sun for years and years. Or, was he maybe the sterile one?

Take Rebecca, wife of Abraham's son, Isaac. Rebecca

was so nice and so full of promise that Isaac could believe neither his eyes, nor his hands. She was, however, just as barren as Sarah. Or was it Isaac's fruitlessness?

Recall Isaac's son, Jacob, and his wife, Rachel. When Jacob saw her for the first time, his heart jumped almost up into his throat. Her womb, too, remained empty, totally empty.

All those wombs remained empty, dry, and barren until God intervened. Infertility seems to be the fate of this world and its humanity, a world resembling that other childless woman in the Old Testament, Hannah, wife of Elkanah, son of Elihu, son of Tohu, son of Zuph the Ephraimite. She went to the temple to pray. She, too, seemed to be without hope. She prayed and prayed and prayed for days, for weeks, until she lost her voice.

Then, the prophet Eli saw her one morning. She was only able to whisper by that time. Eli said, "Get out, you are drunk!" She answered, "I am not drunk, I am desperate." She continued praying, and she was heard. God intervened.

All through the Old Testament the pious ones prayed, "O God, raise your power and come to our help!" This is a rather tame translation of a much more powerful text, "O God, raise your potency, and give us life!" This prayer is not the end of the story in the Bible. It is not the end of its history. This prayer was not the end for any of the women we have mentioned. In all cases God came to help, to give life. In as far as we are concerned, God already did this long ago.

Paul wrote several times, "Don't forget that you already received the new life!" We need not pray for it as if we had not yet received it. We have it. It is only a question of giving birth to its fruits."

The new life is no longer a dream, an utopia. It is a growing realization. We live in the time of its coming, its advent.

The Story of the Well

We all know the story of Jesus at the well near Samaria. The story is very common. It belongs to a genre found in all types of literature. A man meets a woman at a well. There is the helping hand of the woman, there is the helping hand of the man, and all that follows thereafter.

The Bible tells the story several times. There is, for instance, the story about Abraham who was looking for a wife for his son Isaac. He sent a trusted servant to the region from which he originally came. The servant arrived in the evening. He went to the local well, fastened his camels and waited for the women of the region to come for water. Before they came, he fell on his knees and prayed, "God of Abraham, here I am standing at this well. I will ask the maidens who come to fetch water to give me something to drink, and I will take her who gives me some water. Take care, please, that she will be the right one" (Genesis 24:12–14). And he waited.

When the women came, he asked them for water. Rebecca gave him some. Immediately he brought out all his treasures, his earrings and a golden nose ring. Rebecca followed him to marry Isaac and became very happy.

There is the story about Jacob, Isaac's son. He was looking for a wife. He, too, went to the local water well. The well was in a pit; on top of it was a very heavy lid, a stone no one was able to take off alone. When Rachel arrived, Jacob's admiration for her was so strengthening that he rolled the lid away without difficulty. The happiness of that evening continued all through their lives.

The third story is about Moses. In the desert he defended the seven daughters of the priest, Reuben, against some ruffians. That event takes place at a well. Moses met his wife, Zipporah, in that way.

Finally, Jesus arrived at a well. Jesus asked a woman for water, and she asked him for the living water that would quench all thirst once and for all. The Gospel of John gives the woman no name, signifying she is representing the whole of humanity, while asking her question.

Jesus and the woman exchange words like Messiah, salvation, and the last things. Give us the living water, give us the water of a new life! Give us salvation!

What was humanity really asking for at that moment? What did Jesus want? What do his followers want? At least two answers seem to be possible.

First is the answer of the group of theologians and faithful who say that Jesus' message is about a heaven to come after our life in this world. That is what we, being washed in the blood of the Lamb, should be waiting for. Jesus came to bring us a spiritual kind of peace of mind in the troubles of this world. They say we should be looking for the end of this aeon. The Kingdom will come at the other side of reality, after this life, in heaven.

They are participating in the commemoration of Jesus' last supper in order not to forget what is waiting for us later—the heavenly banquet. They are looking more up to heaven, than around themselves in this world. Their orientation is vertical.

A second group believes that Jesus' message is about the liberation of the oppressed and the rehabilitation of the poor. According to them, it is about justice, equality and community here on earth. Jesus can be found neither in piety nor in prayer groups. We have to look for him in the slum areas of our world, such as among the banana plantations of Central America and the tea pickers in Africa.

Both groups of thinkers are facing difficulties. The first group, with the apparently more pious interpretation, has no identity problem at all. They know what it means to be a Christian. They know what makes their group different from all the others. They are willing to witness, if need be, night and day, about Jesus and their trust in him. Their Christian identity is not the difficulty. The problem is their relevance to our world. What is the significance of their piety to others? What would change in *this* world if everyone would believe in Jesus in their way?

For the second group that relevance is no problem. They have a clear idea of what they want. They are working for the liberation and emancipation of the oppressed and the poor. They are teaching illiterate people how to read and to write. They are organizing legal assistance for the rightless ones. They are members of organizations like Amnesty International. They do all kinds of things in the environment in which we live. They, however, have difficulties with their

Christian identity. Aren't others doing the same things as they are doing?

In Japan a group of students at the Meiji Gakuin University went so far in this second interpretation of the Christian salvation that they broke down their own University Chapel to use the stones and wood to build houses for the poor.

What Is Salvation?

What was humanity asking for at that well near Samaria? The polarization we described above can be found wherever churches organize themselves. It is not only a question of some individuals or of some small groups. It is an issue that has divided the whole of the churches' activities and life.

In 1975 two international church organizations met in Nairobi—the World Council of Churches and the International Council of Christian Churches. The two groups differed in their interpretation of Jesus' mission here on earth. It is about heaven, or is it about this world?

In 1980 a similar ambiguity arose when the World Council of Churches organized its World Conference on Mission in Melbourne, which was followed a few weeks later by an International Conference on practically the same issue, organized by the Evangelicals in Pattaya, Thailand.

What to do? How to answer our question? Would it be possible to harmonize the "horizontal" and "vertical" dimensions to Christianity?

The problem seems to arise from a misunderstanding of the two "moments" in our history—the moment of creation and the instant of our recreation. God created humanity in terrific power together with the whole of the world. This work extends to the whole of our horizontal network of relatedness. It is a work begun by God and entrusted to us.

The Indian theologian, Choan-Seng Song, wrote, "The act of creation, we may say, is a political act. It is a manifestation, organization and mobilization of power for a certain definite purpose in the ordering of human society."

He added, "Obviously this is a platitude."

One might wonder whether that is true. It seems that under the influence of our justifiable interest in our redemptive salvation as brought by Jesus Christ, we forget about creation and the powers it left in us. We neglect the original innate dynamism in us and the imperishable Spirit we received at the moment of our creation. We lost much of our respect for the divine sparks of energy that made us develop the variety of cultures we live in.

True, Jesus came to save us "from on high." In this way he reconnected us over a vertical line with the Father. He blew a new breath of life into us; but it is only when we consider and live our creation and salvation together that we will find a solution to the dilemma of "horizontal" and "vertical," of "context" and "text" in our personal and communal lives.

Human life encompasses the past, the present, and the future. Human life is a totality. In a sense, this is not an adequate expression. Though past, present, and future hang together, life is not really a totality. It is not something accomplished. It is not closed-ended. It is open-ended—open in the direction of the future, but also open in the direction of the past. What will happen to us influences what has happened to us. It is that double openness we have to realize in the present. Creation, salvation, recreation, redemption, and fulfillment all go together.

They did so for Jesus, the God-man among us:

He opened his mouth and said, "Abba, Amen," thus recreating the whole of humanity in one family.

He took his food and his drink, sharing it, and said, "Do this," thus recreating the whole of the old economic order.

He said, "No one among you should be called Lord, master, or father," thus recreating the whole of the political order.

He took a child and placed it in their midst, thus recreating the cultural order and declaring himself and us responsible for the poor and the oppressed.

He said, "Look at the flowers of the field and the birds of the air," thus recreating our ruined ecological order.

He died on the cross and rose in glory—alleluiah, thus recreating the meaning of human life.

He breathed his Spirit into us, thus recreating our past in the present, in view of our common future.

Indeed, if we are his followers, we should cooperate with the renewed creational dynamism in us. That must have been what he meant when he said, "Do this to commemorate me."

NOTES

1. Dietrich Bonhoeffer, *Creation and Fall* (New York: MacMillan, 1965).

2. Robin Horton, *African Traditional Thought and Western Science* (Africa, 1967). Vol. 37, No. 1: pp 50-71; No. 2: pp 155-187.

3. Sir James Frazer, *The Golden Bough* (1890, repr. New York: St. Martin Press, Inc., 1980).

4. William James, *The Varieties of Religious Experience* (1902, repr. New York: Penguin Books, 1982).

5. Edward Schillebeeckx, *Jesus, An Experiment in Christology* (New York: Crossroad, 1981).

6. Placide Tempels, *Bantu Philosophy* (Paris: Presence Africaine, 1959).

7. David B. Barrett, Ed., *World Christian Encyclopedia, A Comparative Survey of Christian Religion in the Modern World A.D. 1900 to 2000* (New York: Oxford University Press, Inc., 1982).

8. David B. Barrett, "A.D. 2000: 350 Million Christians in Africa," *International Review of Mission*, Vol. 49, No. 1 pp 39-44 (Published at Geneva by the Commission on World Mission and Evangelism of the World Council of Churches, 1970).

9. These studies were started at the Department of Philosophy and Religious Studies of the University of Nairobi, Kenya (East Africa), by staff and students in 1972).

10. Schillebeeckx, *Ibid.*

11. Choan-Seng Song, *Christian Mission in Reconstruction, An Asian Analysis* (New York: Orbis Books, 1977).

12. This data is taken from *The New International Economic Disorder*, Comment No. 47 (London: Catholic Institute of International Relations, 1983).

13. Maurice Nedoncelle, *God's Encounter with Man* (New York: Sheed and Ward, 1964).

14. Ernest E. Larkin and Gerald T. Broccolo, Editors, "Spiritual Renewal of the American Priesthood" (Washington: National Conference of Catholic Bishops, Publication Office NCCB, 1976).